FOR THE FAMILY'S SAKE

Lottie H Leslie.
June/80

FOR THE FAMILY'S SAKE

A History of the Mothers' Union 1876-1976

OLIVE PARKER

MOWBRAYS
LONDON & OXFORD

ISBN: 0 264 66258 X *(paperback)*
     0 264 66343 8 *(hardback)*

Typeset in 11 on 12pt Monotype Baskerville series 169
by Cotswold Typesetting Ltd. and printed in Great Britain
by Lowe & Brydone (Printers) Ltd., Thetford, Norfolk

First published by A. R. Mowbray & Co. Limited,
The Alden Press, Osney Mead, Oxford OX2 OEG
in association with the Mothers' Union

CONTENTS

PREFACE

THROUGHOUT its history the Mothers' Union has aroused strong feelings both for and against what it has set out to do. It would be possible to write about it from many points of view. What I have tried to do is to enter into its life as it developed, using wherever possible the words of its members and of those involved in its affairs.

For this I am indebted at every point to a succession of editors of Mothers' Union publications. I cannot thank them all but I can express my gratitude to the present editors, to Mrs Peggy Slemeck of *Mothers' Union News* and to Mrs Mary Thompson of *Home and Family*.

In the historical sections I have relied heavily on Violet Lancaster's *A Short History of the Mothers' Union* (published by the Mothers' Union, 1958, 20p) and *George and Mary Sumner, Their Life and Times* by Joyce Coombs (The Sumner Press, 1965, £1.25). I am also indebted to the memoir of Mary Sumner by Mrs Horace Porter, last reprinted in 1950 by the Mothers' Union.

New Dimensions; The Report of the Bishop of Willesden's Commission on the Objects and Policy of the Mothers' Union (SPCK, 1972, £1.00) not only provided material for Chapter 12 but proved a useful summary of facts and opinions for the recent history of the society.

My task has only been possible through the generous co-operation of Mrs Farnill, the Central Secretary, and the staff at The Mary Sumner House. I must mention in particular Miss Mollie Crowder who not only packed innumerable parcels of archives and ferreted out pieces of information when I clamoured for them, but has over the years sustained me by her affection and understanding.

This book is offered to the many friends I have made in the Mothers' Union with the hope that it might be of some use as the society moves into its next century of witness and service.

Authors by tradition render thanks to their spouses and I can be no exception. 'Mothers' Union husbands' have been a necessary feature of the society's life from George Sumner onwards. Mine has known the drawbacks of living with a wife whose head is full of great matters. I hope he has also experienced some of the advantages that have come to a multitude of families through the existence of the Mothers' Union.

April 1975   *Olive Parker*
                                          Portree, Isle of Skye

THE BEGINNING

'One long period of unalloyed happiness'

PIONEERS who leave behind them movements that continue to make their mark on the world are not always remarkable for the happiness of their personal lives. They are often angry people, incensed by the abuses they see around them. They are made impatient by the lack of understanding which greets their vision. They chafe at the gap between their ideals and things as they are.

Mary Sumner was exceptional. Her long life began with happiness, was fulfilled in a contented marriage and ended in the assurance of an unruffled faith in a life hereafter.

By a fortunate chance, there is in existence a description of the home where as Mary Heywood she spent her happy childhood. When she was four years old in 1832, her father gave up his banking interests in Manchester and bought Hope End, a house in rural Hertfordshire, from the infamous Mr Barrett.

Sixty years later Mary Sumner looked back over her memories. 'My first recollections of the new home which became so unspeakably dear to us all was the account given by some of the old servants, of Elizabeth Barrett's agony of grief and her bitter tears, in driving away from Hope End. I felt so sorry for her, and I guarded, with a sort of loyal sympathy, her favourite flowers in her little garden up by the large walled kitchen garden, and thought how too happy I was to live in such a lovely home while she was pining somewhere far away.'

The lines of Elizabeth Barrett's poem *Aurora Leigh* describe

not only her own childhood experience but that of Mary
Heywood, the little girl who followed her at Hope End.

> 'Green the land is where my daily
> Steps in jocund childhood played,
> Dimpled close with hill and valley,
> Dappled very close with shade;
> Summer snow of apple blossoms
> Running up from glade to glade.
> The trees were interwoven wild,
> And spread their boughs enough about
> To keep both sheep and shepherd out,
> But not a happy child.'

There were three children in the Heywood household.
Thomas was educated at home with Margaret, the older
girl, and Mary until he was sent to Eton. Their upbringing
became the main preoccupation of their parents. In a household with adequate domestic help, the Heywoods found
themselves with considerable leisure which they largely
devoted to their children. Both Mr and Mrs Heywood were
singularly qualified for the task of developing the young
minds in their care.

Thomas Heywood had been known in Lancashire not
only as an astute business man but as a man of letters with a
background of wide reading and a comprehensive knowledge
of local history. This is how his daughter Mary remembered
him: 'If we drove or walked with him, he used to tell us
long historical stories so graphically that I felt as if I had
assisted personally at the battles of Crecy and Agincourt,
talked to the Black Prince, and seen the Duke of Wellington
at Waterloo.'

The Heywood children were expected to get to terms with
the world beyond Hope End. Foreign governesses taught
them French, German and Italian. Every year the family
lumbered about the continent in heavily laden horse-drawn
carriages. Mary was only seven when she was first taken on
these safaris and found much that was distinctly wearisome.

'My father wished us each to write a journal, and I can recall my first journal-book, with the big round hand recording with difficulty and exceeding dullness small details of no interest.'

The children were not always models of decorum, especially when mounted on their ponies, as Mary Sumner recalled. 'Our joy was to gallop about the park together, leaping ditches and flying over fences, often without saddles.' When the young Tom, whom Mary adored, led her in a wild career over hedge and ditch, her father's hair 'stood somewhat on end', she remembered.

Mrs Heywood was at the quiet centre of this lively household. When Mary Sumner tried to set down on paper memories of her early life she said, 'Concerning my mother, I feel it more difficult to write.' Steady goodness and simple faith that Mrs Heywood seems to have possessed in abundance are unforgettable to those in touch with them and impossible to describe adequately. Mary Sumner found one phrase that brings them alive. 'There was no *parenthesis* in her religion. It moulded her whole tone of thought and manner of life.'

Mary's every day began when her mother gathered the children round her for Bible reading and prayers. 'What a debt of gratitude we owe her for this! It has helped us through life, for what is learned in childhood is never forgotten.'

But, however devout, Mrs Heywood was the mother of two girls who, as they grew up, must be introduced into society. In 1846 she took them to Rome for the winter. Margaret had become engaged to her cousin as soon as her age allowed. Mary, who had a good voice and enjoyed showing off, was fired with ambition to sing in grand opera. Not quite eighteen, she plunged into parties and concerts, sight-seeing by day and visiting the English community in the evenings. She was pretty and healthy, still slender and with bright intelligent eyes.

It was not long before she met George Sumner at the house of one of their friends. From then on, he became a regular escort of the Heywood ladies. The thought of a career in opera vanished from Mary's mind. She knew now what she wanted in her life. George Sumner seems to have been equally certain that he wanted Mary from the start of their acquaintance. He was wintering in Rome between coming down from Oxford and entering on his life as an Anglican clergyman. He was following a strong family tradition by becoming ordained. He was connected with several Archbishops of Canterbury. His father was Bishop of Winchester, in those days a huge diocese which included most of the Home Counties. His home was Farnham Castle.

The alliance was greeted with enthusiasm by both families. Eighteen months after they met in Rome, the Bishop came to marry his son to Mary Heywood in Hope End's parish church. The sun shone on a splendid Victorian occasion. The bride went to her wedding between banners wishing her joy and arches made of summer flowers with some six hundred tenants and employees to cheer her on her way.

The young couple made their first home at Crawley. George Sumner was hardly typical of the usual young curate. When he was ordained, he had been appointed chaplain to his uncle, the Archbishop of Canterbury. The bishop of the parish where he was serving was his father with whom he had always had close ties. This curacy lasted only a few months. Within the year George Sumner's mother died. His father was everwhelmed with grief in the echoing emptiness of Farnham Castle. George took his wife and their new baby to live there, trying to fill some of the void his mother's death had created.

This was not a period when personal relationships between married couples were subjected to public scrutiny; nor were the young Sumners the kind of people who would indulge in detailed discussion of their domestic life. Mary

Sumner was to describe her marriage in later years as 'one long period of unalloyed happiness'. One thing is certain. The birth of a child was of immense significance to them and, through them, to a great many other people. As she herself said:

'It has always seemed to me that the first thought about the Mothers' Union dawned upon me in the early years of my happy married life, when our eldest child was born. I shall never forget the awful sense of responsibility which seemed to overwhelm me as I took her in my arms, and realised that God had given an immortal soul into our keeping.

'As I gazed with rapture at my little baby, it struck me how much I needed special teaching for so great a work as the character-training of a child, and how little I knew about it. I felt that mothers had one of the greatest and most important professions in the world, and yet there was no profession which had so poor a training for its supreme duties.'

It is easy for modern readers to miss the significance of what Mary Sumner was saying. An awful sense of responsibility meant that she was in the throes of an authentic religious experience, filled with awe at the magnitude of the work God had entrusted to her in bringing up a human being to know and love her Creator.

As for talk of motherhood being a profession for which training was needed, this was unheard of among women of her sort. They did not consider themselves as concerned in any way with professions. Training children was left to governesses and maids. The ladies considered themselves true amateurs in all things.

Three years after their marriage, the Bishop must have considered that the young couple should have their own life for he installed George Sumner in the living of Old Alresford, a scattered village not far from Winchester. Mary Sumner embarked joyfully on creating her own home in which her children could grow up as happily as she had done at Hope End.

The rectory which was to be home to the Sumners for the next thirty-four years was on a scale that modern incumbents would find daunting. Reception rooms were large and elegantly furnished. The rector had a fine study on the first-floor. There were rambling kitchen quarters, several outbuildings and sixteen bedrooms. The main bedroom is now the chapel of a retreat and conference house. The nuns who minister to the needs of their guests are carrying on the tradition Mary Sumner established of an ordered prayerful way of life.

Her debt to the ménage at Hope End is easy to trace. Family and servants were gathered together for daily prayers and Bible study. The Sumners had three children who occupied a large part of their mother's time and thought. She was also eager to help her husband who was a conscientious parish priest. 'I had no leisure,' she said later, 'for work outside our home and parish.' To her children as they grew up, the rectory was a place they were always to remember with affection. No grumbling was allowed, her daughter recalled. 'She said it was like the east wind in a house.'

George Sumner seems to have been less in evidence as a factor in his children's education but he had his job to do in the parish. There is evidence that he was fond of small children. At the end of his life one of his greatest pleasures was visiting the school he and Mary Sumner had built in Winchester from their own money and talking to the pupils there.

At Old Alresford he taught regularly in the parish schools and took seriously his responsibility for the spiritual training of the pupils. He took a practical interest in adult education and endowed the village with a library and reading room, not at all a usual feature at that time. He was an assiduous visitor in the homes of his people, making special calls when there was special need and calling at hours when he would find the men at home as well as the women and children. He was a mild-natured man, not caring for the controversies that were a feature of the Church of England at that time. He was a faithful pastor, careful to take regular services in his churches and concerned to bring home to his flock the practical applications of the Christian gospel.

This was the great age of parish meetings. Many church organisations began in the middle of the nineteenth century and the Sumners took them up with enthusiasm. Sunday Schools flourished. In Old Alresford there were also evening classes for the children who had to be sent out to work early. A branch of the Church of England Temperance Society was started to combat the evil of alcoholism that was a blight of the poorer families of the day.

The rector held meetings of the Young Men's Association and ran successful Men's Bible Classes. Mary Sumner was often in demand to extend her skill in telling Bible stories from the smaller circle of her own family. There were special meetings for the 'cottage mothers', as they didn't appear to mind being called, for married men, and even a garden society to help beautify the village and encourage the growing of vegetables.

It would be easy to write off the Sumners as part of the comfortable middle-class who soothed their consciences with a little first-aid while the working-classes suffered unheeded all around, but it would be mistaken. Though they were not revolutionaries by nature or upbringing, they seem to have understood the lives of the farm labourers in the miserable cottages in the parish and felt with them in their troubles. They spent a lot of time and energy on doing all they could think of to be of service to them.

It would be equally mistaken to see them as isolated from intellectual movements of the time. Anglican clergy were still part of the mainstream of English society with a self-confidence in their position that has been lost as the Christian Church has become an embattled minority. The Sumners entertained and were entertained by a wide circle of friends. They met Carlyle, Thackeray and Kingsley. Heywood Sumner, their son, married into the Benson family. When Mary Sumner came to want someone to edit a magazine, she had no hesitation in approaching Charlotte Yonge, one of the best-known novelists of the period.

In 1876 Mary Sumner was almost fifty years old. Margaret, her eldest daughter, had married her cousin and was herself a mother. Perhaps because Mary Sumner found herself with more leisure, she looked round her husband's parish and wondered if she could do more for the women who were still bringing up their families. Perhaps the experience of being a grandmother had brought back to her mind the feelings of inadequacy as well as rapture when she was first a mother herself.

Whatever the exact reasons, she decided to summon the mothers of Old Alresford to a meeting in her drawing-room. They came on a day when the long windows were open onto the summer garden. The 'cottage women' arrived on foot, neat in best clean cotton. Well-dressed matrons descended from carriages. They sat down together and waited.

Mothers' Union workers up to the present day cherish the story that at this point Mary Sumner took fright. Not able to face the women she had summoned, she went to her husband and begged him to speak to them. It was only the following week when they re-assembled that she found the courage to tell them what was in her mind. She would herself in later years encourage the timid by this account of her own fearfulness at embarking on a new piece of service for her Master.

The reasons for her intense nervousness are not immediately obvious. She was used to public occasions. She often sang for her friends. She was an old hand at speaking to meetings in the parish, to men, women and children of all ages. We can only speculate. Did she find the amalgamation of women from her own social sphere with the women she visited in their cottages suddenly overwhelming? Was she aware that she had launched something without being entirely certain what it was? Is it fanciful to wonder if she had a presentiment that she was letting herself in for arduous and demanding leadership of the great movement that would spring from this small beginning?

Whatever the cause she had recovered herself when the women assembled again. Regular meetings started and were to continue in the rectory for the nine years before the Sumners moved on to other spheres of work.

The only evidence of what happened at those early meetings is a card Mary Sumner drew up. Fifty copies were printed. The prayer she suggested for daily recitation became, with a few small alterations, the official prayer of the Mothers' Union. Her particular mixture of piety and practical common-sense comes through clearly.

'Remember that your children are given up, body and soul, to Jesus Christ in Holy Baptism, and that your duty is to train them for His service.

Try by God's help to make them truthful, obedient and pure.

Never allow coarse jests, bad angry words, or low talk in your house.

Speak gently.

You are strongly advised never to give your children beer, wine or spirits without the doctor's orders, or to send young people to the public-house.

Do not allow your girls to go about the streets at night, and keep them from unsafe companions and from any dangerous amusement.

Be careful that your children do not read bad books or police reports.

Set them a good example in word and deed.

Kneel down and pray morning and evening, and teach your children to pray.

Try to read a few verses of the Bible daily, and come to church as regularly as possible.

If you repent truly of your sins, and desire with all your heart to love and follow the Lord Jesus, come to the Holy Communion, and feed on Him by faith, then will your souls be strengthened and refreshed. Jesus said, "Do this in remembrance of me", it was His dying command.

Ask and it shall be given you; seek and ye shall find; knock and it shall be opened unto you.

St Matt. vii. 7

PRAYER TO BE SAID DAILY

O Lord, give me Thy Holy Spirit, that I may firmly believe in Jesus Christ, and love Him with all my heart. Wash my soul in His Precious Blood. Make me to hate sin and to be holy in thought, and word, and deed. Help me to be a faithful wife, and a loving mother. Bless me and unite us together in love and prayer, and teach me to train my children for Heaven. Pour our Thy Holy Spirit on my dear husband and children. Make our Home, a Home of peace and love, and may we so live on earth, that we may live with Thee for ever in Heaven, for Jesus Christ's sake. *Amen.*'

There is no firsthand evidence of how the women of Old Alresford responded to these meetings though the fact that they persisted over the years shows that they were valued. The wives must have talked about what was going on for the men of the parish were soon asking if they could have something of the sort themselves.

On Sunday evenings George Sumner took a service in a remote part of his parish. He was delighted with the suggestion that his wife should hold meetings for fathers while he was busy elsewhere. At seven o'clock each Sunday evening between thirty and forty men came to the rectory. Her methods seem to have been much the same with the men as with their wives. They studied the Bible together, discussing its meaning for them. Into this, she reports, they 'entered heartily'. She would talk of a father's share in the responsibility for training children. Such teaching must have seemed strange in an age when homes and children were considered women's business.

Mary Sumner enjoyed those Sunday evenings. 'A most delightful gathering', she said. Again she speaks of her initial fears in facing a new venture. 'Although at first I was intensely alarmed at taking such a meeting of men, I soon found it a real pleasure. They were so kind, grateful, and responsive.'

She has left an account of one occasion which gives a glimpse of her charm and lightness of touch. Above all she demonstrates the warmth of her human sympathies. 'I ventured on one occasion to speak to the men about their married lives, and I told them, with a smile, that they doubtless said many pretty things to their wives before they were married, and they ought to show love and courtesy to them afterwards.

'I urged each of them to give a little present to his wife on her birthday. The hint was taken, and the wife of one of them, when next I called on her, told me that her husband had bought her a lovely shawl, and on her birthday he put it round her shoulders and gave her his good wishes with a kiss. She said, "I couldn't help crying for joy, because he had never done such a thing or spoken so lovingly to me since we were married." '

2

EXPANSION

'Let us appeal to the mothers of England'

IN nineteenth-century England forces were gathering that were hostile to the Church. Cities, swollen with families coming from the countryside to seek work, seethed with talk of rebellion. Land workers chafed under the repressive yoke of squire and parson. The Church of England took counter measures. Church Congresses were held in various centres, partly as a show of strength and partly in an attempt to communicate its message.

One such congress was held in Portsmouth in 1885. Because the women of the day were beginning to assert their separate identity as human beings with their own needs and problems, an afternoon meeting for women was included in the programme. Matters were in the hands of a visiting bishop, Ernest Wilberforce. His wife has given an account of what happened.

'My husband (then Bishop of Newcastle) had been asked to preside at this particular meeting, and as we came into the hall, which was packed to overflowing the sight which met us moved him profoundly. On all sides there were rows upon rows of women, many of them with sad, anxious faces, or bearing some unmistakable sign of poverty's cold grip, and he felt that a woman could probably speak to them with a greater power of sympathetic understanding than even the best of the appointed speakers, who were all men.

'That seemed the natural arrangement for such an occasion forty years ago. Women had not yet taken up the work of public speaking, and it was a sudden and quite unusual resolve that the Bishop took—in the truest sense, as I believe, an "inspiration of the moment"—when he went straight to Mrs Sumner, our friend of many years' standing, and asked her to speak. She held up her hands in horror at the idea of such a thing, and her refusal was prompt and emphatic.

'Nothing daunted, he still pleadingly insisted, and upon her protesting that her husband would particularly dislike her speaking in public, the Bishop undertook to make it all right with him.

'Finally, placing his hands on Mrs Sumner's shoulders, my husband gave her his blessing, and said that for that occasion he was her Bishop, and therefore able to lay his commands upon her. Her hesitation was all put behind her then, and she set herself to obey the call quite simply, although "with a trembling heart," as she herself wrote afterwards.

'After this touching little incident we proceeded to the platform, Mrs Sumner sitting behind the Chairman, who called upon her before the meeting closed. He told the audience that a woman who cared for them, and wanted to help them in the trials and difficulties of daily life, would now speak to them. She came forward and spoke for a few minutes with all the charm and earnestness that thereafter characterised all her utterances, while we who listened felt that the Holy Spirit was manifestly guiding and strengthening her in an undertaking which at that time called for no little courage.'

Mary Sumner began:

'At the present moment the eyes of England are directed in a very special manner upon the women. It is said that there is in many cases a very terrible want of morality and high tone in the homes and among the people of this country, and the question is *What can be done to raise the national character?* The answer is *Let us appeal to the mothers of England.* It is the Mothers who can in great measure work the reformation of the country.'.

She went on to set out the idea of a movement that had
been growing in her mind over the years in Old Alresford.
'My friends, as wives and mothers, we have a great work to
do for our husbands, our children, our homes and our
country, and I am convinced that it would greatly help if we
could start a Mothers' Union, wherein all classes could unite
in faith and prayer, to try to do this work for God.'

The women in her audience responded with such enthusiasm that these few minutes became the main topic of conversation at the Congress. The leading personalities with
their wives met at dinner that evening. Mary Sumner,
entirely at her ease in this setting, told them of her women's
meetings in Old Alresford and her idea of expanding the
work among mothers until they became a power for good in
the land. 'Union is strength,' she declared.

Next day there was a gathering of ladies in the Close at
Winchester. They soon agreed to establish this new Mothers'
Union as an organisation in the Winchester diocese. The
Bishop when approached was enthusiastic. Mary Sumner
was the obvious choice as diocesan president.

She was herself about to set up house in the Close. George
Sumner had just been appointed a residential canon. As
Archdeacon of Winchester, his main job would be travelling
round the sprawling diocese inspecting the charges. His wife
could go with him, establishing branches of the new society.
Mary Sumner, nearing sixty, was by now a matronly figure
with white hair, bright eyes and a sweet smile. As her three
children had homes of their own, she was ready to give her
time and abundant energy to the work opening out before
her.

It was not only in the Winchester diocese that Mary
Sumner's help and advice was sought. Even before she had
spoken at Portsmouth, friends of hers had been copying
what she was doing at Old Alresford. Mrs Maclagan, for
instance, had launched her own meetings in Lichfield on
similar lines.

After the 1885 Church Congress, inquiries came thick and fast. Only two years later Mary Sumner was telling the first Mothers' Union Diocesan Conference to be held in Winchester that the diocese had fifty-seven branches with eleven more under way. Seventeen other dioceses had taken up the idea and numbers of people wrote daily for information. No wonder her family remembered her as always having a pen in her hand when she was at home.

The rate of expansion was astonishing. By 1890, only five years on from Portsmouth, a progress report tells of Mothers' Union branches in practically every English diocese and says that 'off-shoots of the Society are making their way in the Colonies, in a variety of distant lands, where English people have settled'.

Eighty years later, when a Commission was studying the future of the society, its members looked back on this period. 'The story of its rise in the thirty years before the First World War can hardly be paralleled outside the pages of the Acts of the Apostles.'*

By 1888 the burden of communicating with members and inquirers was beyond even Mary Sumner's busy pen. A monthly *Mothers' Union Journal* made its appearance and reached a circulation of 13,000 in two years. Its readership was in the main the 'cottage mothers' who were flooding in to the society in great numbers. It carried a mixture of practical advice ('a great many nice serges are made now, all wool and as low as a shilling a yard') and moral exhortation. ('Mothers! you cannot tell how much good you may do by teaching your children wise lessons.')

Two years later it was joined by a magazine designed for 'mothers of the high classes', called *Mothers in Council*. Mary Sumner persuaded her Hampshire neighbour, Charlotte Yonge, to become its first editor. She would be granted, Mary Sumner considered, a 'respectful hearing'. The practical advice given here is rather different. 'Make the girls

New Dimensions, p. 15.

run about for your handkerchief and your cologne.' The
problems created by careless servants loom large. 'A young
relation of mine narrowly escaped death in consequence of
his mother's nurse giving him an overdose of opium to
counteract other drugs which she had taken upon herself to
administer.'

In a variety of ways the message was constantly being
driven home. Mothers have a sacred charge to help their
children to spiritual maturity. By uniting together they can
strengthen each other and become a power for good in a
world that needs what they have to give. The backbone of
the work was regular meetings of members in their parishes.
When Mrs Maclagan's husband was translated from Lichfield to York, she continued to found Mothers' Union
branches. She describes the meetings: 'The women are very
responsive. They will walk any distance in any weather to
attend the meeting, and after it is over crowd round the
speaker to purchase cheap tracts and letters of advice on the
training of children. They often ask afterwards if "that lady"
will come and speak to them again. When one considers
their many difficulties, it is really touching to hear of the
efforts they make to follow the advice given to improve the
sanitary conditions of their houses ... and to learn as
mothers of England their great responsibilities.'

'Lady mothers' would be invited to gatherings in a drawing
room which had a twofold purpose, to bring home to them
their own responsibilities for their children and to train
future leaders for the work of the society.

In 1890, for example, 500 potential leaders were invited to
Farnham Castle. George Sumner, who was by this time
Bishop of Guildford, was there with his wife. Charlotte
Yonge was one of the speakers. Though Mary Sumner considered her a poor orator and somewhat careless of her
appearance, she realised the value of such a name on the
programme. A duchess and a dowager marchioness also
addressed the gathering.

This was only one date in Mary Sumner's heavy load of meetings, travelling and correspondence. When she looked back, she admitted that 'the strain of those first years was sometimes not far from breaking her down'. 'It would probably have done so altogether but that she never increased it by thinking how great it was or how much she was doing or had still to do', Mrs Porter recalls.

The tremendous rate of growth brought huge problems. Nobody had created the machinery for what was almost at once a nation-wide movement and soon got a foothold overseas. The only card of membership was the one given to the women who came to the first meetings in Old Alresford Rectory. The only official body was the Winchester Diocesan Council set up by the ladies of the Close.

The Mothers' Union in the London diocese took a hand. By 1892 there was sufficient support for a diocesan committee to be functioning with the bishop's wife as president. It summoned representatives of other dioceses to meet for discussion of mutual concerns in Church House, Westminster. This paved the way for annual conferences. By 1896 a Central Council was in existence which set about formulating a central policy to hold the rapidly expanding body in a coherent framework.

Three Objects, central to the work, were set down. Archbishops and bishops were invited to become patrons. Every Mothers' Union meeting was to begin with prayer. All official workers must be communicant members of the Church of England. Elections were to take place every three years. A Central President was chosen.

There could be no doubt who that would be. Mary Sumner, though not far off seventy, was as energetic as ever in the cause of the Mothers' Union. But it was becoming essential to share the day-to-day affairs, especially as George Sumner's health was beginning to cause concern. Being with him was becoming more important even than serving the Mothers' Union.

Members of the society were amongst Queen Victoria's most loyal subjects. In 1898 the final human approval was set on their work when the Queen agreed to become patron. Mary Sumner was triumphant. 'The ideal wife and mother of this nation has consented to place herself at our head.'

As the twentieth century came in, the Mothers' Union grew and grew. In one year, 1904, over three hundred branches were started and almost 20,000 women joined. The divorce rate was also on the increase; the 1,098 divorces for this same year was the largest number ever recorded. This was endangering the greatness of England which, Mary Sumner told the Mothers' Union annual meeting, could be attributed to three causes: belief in the Bible, the observance of Sunday and faithful marriage.

A great deal of the impetus still depended on Mary Sumner's personal efforts. She was still constantly writing letters at the table placed so that she could glance up and smile at her husband. When she journeyed, he went with her whenever possible. In 1901 they were in Ireland together, launching the Mothers' Union in new areas and strengthening it where it existed already. The wife of an Irish bishop wrote afterwards: 'It is hard to realise that your visit to Dublin is over. I do thank God for it and feel that it must have brought a blessing personally to those who heard you, and stirred up in them the missionary spirit to extend our Union. I can judge best of its effect on my own members here. I know several mothers who were touched and helped by what you said; and just now a young mother of the working class told me how she and two other of our members had been speaking together and she said, "When she stood up she looked like the Queen, and she went into all the little details, so it made it all so real and such a help to us." And then she told me how she went home and resolved what she would do for her little boy of five.'

Sadness at the inevitable parting in this world was clouding the unalloyed happiness of the Sumners as the old gentleman grew frailer. He gave up his offices one by one, archdeacon, bishop and canon. When he was eighty there was a great party with the cathedral bells ringing out and the many friends this quiet faithful priest had made over the years coming to honour him.

There was another party for their diamond wedding when their own children and children's children were joined in thanksgiving for this marriage by the members of the Mothers' Union, 'our youngest child', as George Sumner used to call it. In 1909 he died, mourned by many women he had never met in many places he would never visit. He was the beloved husband of 'our Foundress', as they called Mary Sumner.

She was getting old herself and was wearied with the strain of personal loss after the years of utter devotion to the cause of the Mothers' Union. The machinery had been set up for others to take over. In 1910 the Dowager Countess of Chichester became Central President in her place. She set about spreading the load among many more shoulders. 'Never again can one individual bear alone the weight and responsibility of the work which has gathered such strength and expansion under her direction.'

Not that Mary Sumner retired from active service there and then. She still kept in close touch with Central Council affairs. She was a leading voice in the cause of religious instruction in schools and campaigned vigorously against proposals for easier divorce. She kept up a vast correspondence with friends known and unknown. Her notes of welcome to new workers or appreciation of service rendered to the cause were treasured by the many who received them. When she emerged to speak at occasional meetings, she had become a celebrity. Mrs Porter tells of one of her last tours, 'a wonderful series of personal triumphs'. She was eighty-four at the time.

'In Southwell, in Newark—where she addressed a large Sunday afternoon gathering of men—Durham, Sunderland,

Carlisle, and all the other northern towns at which she spoke, it was the same story. Crowds of women—often of men also—thronged about her not only in the halls where she spoke, but outside also, in the streets as she came out, and along the road as she drove away; eager to get a touch of the hand if possible, or at least a word, a look a smile.

'The climax was reached at the Mothers' Union Conference in York, where thousands of members of the Union congregated day by day throughout the week. On the afternoon of the great Mass Meetings held simultaneously in different halls, Mrs Sumner drove from one to the other, to say a few words at each, and all who witnessed her course from place to place agree that it was like nothing so much as a royal progress.'

The 1914 war brought suffering on an unimaginable scale. The Mothers' Union shared in the bitterness of the loss of husbands and sons, brothers and fathers. Mary Sumner suffered with her band of mothers, looking out with her warm sympathy from the quiet house in Winchester.

Now she in her turn laid down active work. After thirty years she resigned as diocesan president of the Winchester Mothers' Union. She allowed her family to persuade her that travelling to London in war-time was not a good idea and was content with news brought by friends who came to visit her and with written accounts of the latest doings of the society. In 1917 she made her last visit to London. The Mothers' Union had acquired its own home. A house in Dean's Yard, close to Church House and just behind Westminster Abbey, had been rented. Mary Sumner knelt in the chapel that was dedicated that day and made a short speech at the opening ceremony. Obviously a very old lady, she was still erect with a clear voice and ready smile.

She had a lovely ninetieth birthday, thoroughly enjoying all the letters and telegrams that arrived at the Close. She was specially pleased with a signed photograph of Queen Mary. Flowers came from the Central Council with a message from the Central President, now Mrs Wilberforce. The wife of the bishop who had insisted on Mary Sumner speaking to the women's meeting in Portsmouth in 1885 was now at the head of the society that had been launched that day.

Mary Sumner in her letter of thanks showed that she was still on the job. 'I am living in daily prayer about my beloved Mothers' Union for it has been the great subject of my life to get faithful married life, holy motherhood and reverance for child life, remembering the importance of daily example of parent life, in every home.'

A message of good wishes from her was read to a gathering of members from many parts of the world held during the Lambeth Conference. Another Central President, Mrs Hubert Barclay, came to see her in Winchester. She even managed to address local members in her daughter's garden at Botley in Hampshire where she took care to speak individually to each woman there. But her life was ebbing away. She died in 1921, by now a legend, and was buried next to her husband after a service in a crowded Winchester Cathedral. 'The whole of England seemed to acknowledge and rejoice in what she had done', wrote one who was present.

Even after the passage of half a century, it is not easy to reach an objective judgement about a woman who inspired such devotion. In many ways she is an unlikely figure to found a movement which helped women to realise their power when they unite together. She was a woman of her day, not out to reform society but content to preserve the values of her class. But she had the force that comes from single-minded concentration on the immediate job in hand. She was intensely practical, seeing the next step ahead and finding the best way of achieving it.

She was a woman with plenty of love to give, the great asset of those who have known much happiness themselves.

She treated the spectacular expansion of the Mothers' Union as a widening of her family circle. Those hectic years were sweetened and warmed by the affection she poured out to the women who were answering her call.

She never seems to have doubted the validity of the Christian faith. Her firm and unsullied belief was at the centre of her being and communicated itself to her audiences in simple direct words.

Prayer was no formality to her. It was the root and ground of her being. The first priority of a good home was for her regular prayer and Bible study. She had grown up in such an atmosphere. She established it in the homes she made for her family at Old Alresford and in Winchester. It was this more than anything that she sought to impart to others.

3

JUBILEE 1926

THE Mothers' Union has always loved a celebration. Great churches packed to the roof. Processions of robed clergy and banners carried proudly. Pretty hats and smiling faces. In the summer of 1926, the M.U. set about celebrating fifty years of existence.

Westminster Abbey was invaded by a capacity congregation. The procession of representatives from dioceses at home and overseas was said to be the longest ever seen there. A banner was presented to the Abbey 'in token of our gratitude to Almighty God for the founding of our World-Wide Fellowship by His servant Mary Sumner, and for the many blessings with which He has blessed us through half a century of growth'.

Next day Winchester Cathedral was crammed full. Afterwards the great congregation 'on a bright midsummer day' filed past the grave where Mary Sumner had been laid five years earlier, piling it high with their flowers.

The Royal Albert Hall could have been filled several times over for The Gift, a Pageant of Motherhood, presented by members themselves. The Mothers' Union could draw on a cast of thousands and more were joining every year.

But none of these events was the highlight for those who travelled great distances to London. This was their first opportunity to see the new headquarters, purpose-built for the needs of the Mothers' Union, called, as might be expected, The Mary Sumner House.

When the Central Council was set up in 1896, one of its

For the Family's Sake

first acts was to appoint a secretary to handle its affairs. Mrs Mathew held this post for twelve years. For the first three she seems to have had an uncomfortable existence, her only office being a locker in the basement of Church House. Then she moved to a room which soon proved too small. By 1914, when Mrs Maude had taken over as secretary, the Mothers' Union was renting four rooms in Church House.

Mrs Wilberforce who became Central President in 1915 began to look ahead to the peace when the work of the society would be more than ever essential in re-building a shattered world. She saw that good ideas need a place to bring them into effect. She proposed to the Central Council that they should start working for a house in the centre of London, not only to strengthen and consolidate all the existing work of the Mothers' Union, but to provide space and opportunity for wider constructive and educative work to be undertaken.

There was some doubt as to whether this was the right time to appeal for money but the interest expressed justified the Central Council in launching a Building Fund. The Queen and the Archbishop of Canterbury gave it their support. A letter in *The Times* appealed to 'all those who have the welfare of the Nation at heart'. The target fixed was £50,000, enough in those days to erect a substantial building a stone's-throw from Westminster Abbey.

While looking round for the right site, the Mothers' Union rented a house in Dean's Yard for a trial run. It was this temporary Mary Sumner House that Mary Sumner visited on her last appearance in London when the Bishop of London dedicated its chapel.

Mrs Maude and her increasing staff set up their offices to keep in touch with members, answer queries, send out literature, service committees. From the start the house was the setting for meetings of many kinds. Lectures for 'working women'. Courses of instruction for leaders and speakers. A maternity centre for 'young mothers of the professional classes'.

The practical mothercraft side of the work did not develop in the way that had been hoped. Perhaps the Mothers' Union in conjunction with other public-spirited people concerned for the welfare of families had done its job too well. After discussions with local agencies in Westminster schemes for co-operating in running maternity and child welfare services were found to be unnecessary. The Mothers' Union concentrated on the spiritual and moral aspects of training for parenthood.

When the war ended branches applied themselves to money raising. In 1922 the right site was found and bought for £11,000. Although this left only a small balance in the Building Fund account, the decision was taken to make the new house larger than was needed at the time. Any spare space could be let to bring in extra income until such time as it was needed by the Mothers' Union.

Mary Sumner's daughter, Mrs Gore-Browne, laid the foundation stone in 1923 in the presence of some two thousand people who represented the many thousands who already felt it was their home. Before it was half built, it was already considered too small and a fourth storey was added.

The construction work was held up through a tragic accident to workmen on the site. When a distinguished assembly that included the Princess Royal and the Archbishop of Canterbury met for the opening ceremony, resourceful women had camouflaged its unready state. Richly coloured banners were borrowed from their cathedral homes to cover undecorated walls. There were plants and banks of flowers 'in abundance wherever they could be placed'.

The way the money had been collected was significant. The total cost was just over £50,000, of which only £1,000 had been given from outside the ranks of members. The rest had come from small offerings made by the women themselves, a few shillings here, a few pence there, spared from family budgets that were often very tight indeed.

There began the constant procession of visitors to the Mary Sumner House that has continued to the present day. Royal personages, church dignitaries, figures in public life, overseas visitors and above all a steady stream of Mothers' Union members. They have come in special trains and hired coaches in their hundreds on diocesan and deanery outings. A branch travels together. A member who has occasion to be in London will spend a little time in 'her' Mary Sumner House. Members join in a service in the chapel, buy from the bookshop, consult with members of the staff, have a meal in the restaurant.

Everything here has been given by members. A figure of the Madonna and Child in the entrance hall is in memory of a member's child. The chapel which was furnished as a memorial to husbands and fathers killed in the 1914 war is full of remembrances of members and their families. Even an office chair is marked with the name of the branch or member who gave it.

The Mary Sumner House has changed here and there over the years but its main functions remain constant. Assembly halls and committee rooms for discussing the society's affairs and pursuing training in various spheres of the work. Literature and personal advice are made available on how to put training into practice. There are places to pray, to meet other members, to have meals and a few bedrooms for those engaged on Mothers' Union business.

Though a good deal of floor space is inevitably taken up with desks and typing tables, filing cabinets and accounting machines, the Mary Sumner House has never been merely a set of offices, essential to the work of a big society but hardly inspiring to contemplate. It has always been looked on as their home by a band of women whose concern is home-making. They built it themselves and they have continued to cherish it.

Another event of 1926 was less obviously exciting than keeping jubilee or visiting the Mothers' Union's new London home but it held important significance for the future. The society was granted a Royal Charter. By 1912 those responsible for the work of the Mothers' Union had been forced to take action to safeguard its identity. Mothers' Unions were appearing all over the country and there was no obligation on those using the name to adhere to its original principles. Some legally reognised body was necessary to hold its property and the assets which it was acquiring.

The simple constitution which had been drawn up in 1896 was superseded by a constitution under which the Mothers' Union became an Incorporated Society. It was not long before expansion overseas made a further step necessary to protect its interests outside the United Kingdom. And so in 1926 the Mothers' Union successfully applied for a Royal Charter.

A knowledge of the provisions of this charter which has governed the society's affairs until very recently is essential in understanding its attitudes. Some of the bye-laws and regulations were to form the basis for intense discussion, being passionately defended and bitterly attacked by many people in many places.

Three Central Objects were set out:

1 To uphold the sanctity of marriage.

2 To awaken in all Mothers a sense of their great responsibility in the training of their boys and girls (the Fathers and Mothers of the future).

3 To organise in every place a band of Mothers who will unite in prayer and seek by their own example to lead their families in purity and holiness of life.

Three kinds of membership was defined:

1 Incorporated Members form the governing body of the society. They, like all official workers, must be members of the Church of England or of a Church in communion therewith.

This provision, which first appeared in the 1912 Constitution, had created unexpected difficulties. Before that time membership of the Church of England was laid down for England and Wales and membership of the Church of Ireland for Ireland. Scotland and the colonies were considered exempt from this provision.

When Mary Sumner started Mothers' Union work in Scotland in 1888, Presbyterians were attracted in equal numbers with Episcopalians and were considered members on equal terms. In 1912 overseas clergy were pressing the society to come out as a completely Church of England body. Arrangements were suggested to keep the Scottish Mothers' Union within its ranks. Perhaps, it was thought, delegates with power to vote could be chosen from Scottish Episcopalian members only. No Scottish officials felt that this kind of arrangement would be satisfactory as it would divide Presbyterians from Episcopalians. The Scottish Mothers' Union had to be granted a special relationship as a sister society, a position it still holds. Since 1926 it has accepted different rules of membership and organises its branches rather differently. In 1949 branches of the Mothers' Union itself were started in some of the Scottish dioceses for Episcopalians only.

2 Ordinary membership is open to married women:

(1) who have been baptised, affirm their belief in the principle of infant baptism, and undertake to bring their children (if any) to Holy Baptism.

(2) who accept the teaching contained in the Apostles' Creed.

(3) who are faithful to their marriage vows.

(4) who declare their adherence to the three Central Objects.

3 Associate membership is for unmarried women who wish to support the work of the society.

Bye-Law Six, which was to be often quoted in the years ahead, states: 'Any person as to whose marriage a Decree of Dissolution has been pronounced by a Court of competent jurisdiction, or who shall during the lifetime of a former wife, marry a person whose previous marriage has been so dissolved, shall be ineligible as an Incorporated, Ordinary or Associate Member of the Society, and if a Member, shall cease *ipso facto* to be a Member.'

Separation was not of itself a bar to membership. Unmarried mothers would not be eligible. There should be not less than three months' probation for membership when there must be 'personal and definite instruction in the Three Objects of the Society'.

The government of the Mothers' Union is the concern of the Central Council which elects an Executive Committee to act on its behalf. The Central Council consists of some members elected by the Incorporated Members but the great majority is elected by the diocesan organisations which are affiliated to the society.

Dioceses are left free to make their own rules in accordance with the constitution but the Presiding Member in the deanery and the Enrolling Member in the branch must be called by these names throughout the society. Branches are only to be started 'with the consent of the Incumbent and must be carried on in accordance with his wishes', a provision that appeared first in 1926 and has come under close scrutiny by both members and clergymen from time to time.

All meetings are to open with prayer. 'Branch programmes shall be so arranged that the spiritual character of the Mothers' Union is maintained.' The society is not to be used as a channel for charitable appeals on behalf of other organisations, a regulation that must have eased the lot of many officials beset by all the good causes in the world.

So the identity of the society was defined and its affairs regulated as it set out on the next fifty years. There was much for it to do as it looked around in the many countries where it was in existence. What that work was and how the Mothers' Union met its various demands throughout its history we shall now describe. The spirit in which its members tackled it was given them in their 1926 Charter. The official form of membership card set out there ends with the words:

'I can do all things through CHRIST which strengtheneth me.'

4

PARENTS AND CHILDREN

'A sense of great responsibility'

'TO awaken in Mothers a sense of their responsibility in the training of their boys and girls (the future Fathers and Mothers of England).' Mary Sumner presented this as the main object of her new society. It has stayed much the same ever since.

When it had to be re-stated for the 1896 Constitution, England had clearly been outgrown and Empire was substituted. Also there was a desire to stress that the Mothers' Union had something to offer women of all kinds. 'Mothers of all classes' were specified.

By 1926 the society had grown beyond the British Empire so that had to go. So too had the classes, by then considered old-fashioned. The wording arrived at was: 'To awaken in all Mothers a sense of their great responsibility in the training of their boys and girls, the Fathers and Mothers of the future.'

It was made abundantly clear from the start what the training involved. 'Remember that your children are given up, body and soul, to Jesus Christ in Holy Baptism, and that your duty is to train them for His service', was how the first card of membership began and the prayer to be said daily included the phrase, 'Teach me to train my children for Heaven.'

When the Mothers' Union began the nation was sharply divided into two. The comfortably-off lived as comfortably as they have ever lived. Servants cared for the physical needs of families, cooking large meals and cleaning big houses.

Nursemaids and governesses were employed to look after the children. Even the more conscientious mothers did not as a rule play much part in the everyday lives of their children. Mary Sumner, like her own mother before her, seems to have been an exception. The general duty of a good parent was limited to ensuring that the best available staff was employed to do the job of bringing up the family.

It was hardly surprising that Mary Sumner felt isolated when faced with the challenge, as she saw it, of a new human life to be brought up to the full knowledge of the Christian faith.

When women of her sort contemplated the families in the labourers' cottages and town tenements, they were gazing across a great void. They could only guess dimly what life was like for the great masses on the poverty line. The enthusiasm with which clergy wives and other public-spirited ladies took up the Mothers' Union is tinged with relief. Here is something they could do for the poor apart from taking nourishing food from their kitchens, something that was concerned with the whole well-being of such families.

As one lady put it in 1893:

'Through a Society you can suggest and recommend improvements and alterations, whilst, if you applied these suggestions to the individual personally, you would be dictating offensively. Everyone who visits among the working classes is conscious of feeling that it would be an impertinence when you are visiting Mrs Jones or Mrs Smith to make personal remarks on the dirtiness of her cottage or the untidiness of her children's clothes. You could hardly give the hints which are wanted without making an enemy, whereas, at a Mothers' Union meeting, the outcome of a Society, you can tell a story to illustrate the comfort of a clean cottage, or select some incident in which want of tidiness in dress leads to a delay, and that delay to loss of a train, and the moral lesson is given not to the one but to the many.

'If this be true of minor matters, it is still more true of greater subjects, of intemperance and immorality. The rules, the objects of the Mothers' Union, give an endless opportunity of bringing those purposes of life, which are common to all of us, before the members of the Union. Then, besides what one may call the repressive side of advice, there is the constructive side, the putting together and the building up, and there, I think the opportunities of a Union in its regular meetings is enormous; the chances it gives of directing to a right judgement about things are so numerous.'

Advice and instructions poured out from leaders of the society and from experts who were invited to speak at meetings and to write articles. As the twentieth century succeeded the nineteenth and differences between the classes grew blurred, there was less practical advice on home-making, diet and physical care and an increased insistence on the need for spiritual training in a world which seemed apathetic or hostile.

By 1974 the expert invited to the Mary Sumner House to advise on the development of young adolescents is a consultant psychiatrist. The language he used is different from that of a hundred years earlier but the intention is the same. 'There is certainly a danger that the small self-contained nuclear family may become a place for the generation of neurotic disorders, and such emotional entanglements which prevent the adolescent from reaching true independence and personal autonomy. But such a family need not be that. It may form a safe base from which all members of the family may be able to develop and experience a wider set of relationships, loyalties and activities.'

It soon became obvious that mothers cannot train children without themselves having a firm basis of knowledge. The Mothers' Union set about educating its members. A Central Lending Library was established in 1906 and grew steadily as books were added. Booklists were drawn up on specific subjects and reviews of new books appeared regularly in the society's journals.

Any copy chosen at random shows the variety covered. A 1953 *Workers' Paper* has a notice of a book analysing the current state of theology. 'This book will stimulate readers to face disconcerting facts about the present state of our own religious condition.' Also mentioned are a study in Christian monotheism, 'a profound and learned work' on Christology and a series of short addresses on moral themes designed for young people. 'A survey of woman's position, especially in the home, through the ages' is followed by a book setting out problems encountered in running local authority children's homes. There is a collection of stories about missionaries in North America for 11–14-year-olds and members are encouraged to put their feet up with a beautifully illustrated book on Florence.

While there has continued to be plenty of helpful advice for literate members, there were always the horses who needed help in learning how to drink. Especially in the early years, there were many who had attained motherhood but had had little formal education. Diocesan schemes were drawn up to give basic religious teaching. Speakers and Enrolling Members were themselves expected to study and to share their knowledge with the women in the branches.

One of the main purposes of central premises was to develop the courses of lectures which attracted 'educated mothers' in great numbers. In 1920, for example, more than 1,500 attended a Lent course given by leading theologians. Such study was expected to be taken seriously. There were examinations with certificates granted by the diocesan bishops.

Those who could not come regularly to London had to be catered for, and the Mothers' Union embarked on correspondence courses in a variety of subjects such as church history, the Bible and the Prayer Book, liturgy and the history of the Mothers' Union. Qualified tutors were engaged and the courses are now integrated into the adult education work of the Church of England. Other methods were added

as they became available. Leaflets and discussion papers,
film strips and tape recordings succeeded lantern slides and
wall pictures. Though the membership became more sophis-
ticated, it was still in need of systematic instruction on
matters of belief and faith.

Though parents have the ultimate responsibility in training
their children, schools have a vital part to play. The Mothers'
Union was started in an atmosphere of growing discussion
about the place of denominational teaching in state education. Its annual conference in 1893 heard from Mary
Sumner that parents ought to insist on their children being
given definite church teaching by those who themselves
believed in what they were teaching.

'One object of our Conference today should be to take
counsel together how we, as educated women, may arise and
build the lives of our children, whether at home or at school,
on foundations which will bear the weight of eternity, and
remove so terrible a reproach from this Christian country as
the neglect of the religious teaching and training of children.'
This was no fleeting interest on her part. Both George and
Mary Sumner had taken a close interest in church schools
from the days when they were concerned with those in the
Old Alresford parish. In this same year they had succeeded
in battling with officialdom to build with their own money a
school in one of the Winchester parishes.

They were caught up in the conflict between the traditional views of the Church which considered education to be
its business, and the new Board Schools, the product of
humanistic impatience with poverty and ignorance among
working people. To church leaders like the Sumners education without religious instruction could not be called
education at all. Mary Sumner stoutly defended the position
of the Church in the matter. 'The result of non-sectarian
teaching is to establish a new form of religion in the Board
Schools which has nothing in common with historical
Christianity or any other form of Christianity. By taking

away everything to which someone objected they have left something which is really worthless. They said they would have no creed and no catechism. The result of unsectarian teaching is a colourless residum which is as objectionable to the earnest Christian as it is contemptible to the earnest unbeliever.'

In 1906 Augustine Birrell introduced his Education Bill in the House of Commons. Mary Sumner, in common with other deeply committed church leaders, saw it as an attempt to secularise education. They realised that it might become law, not because it was actively supported by the majority but because people were not aware of its implications. It was in just such a situation that the Mothers' Union seemed designed to act. Mary Sumner alerted it to campaign against the proposed Bill. Meetings for parents were organised up and down the country where speakers set out the dangers and pleaded for corporate resistance to it.

A deputation from the society went to see Augustine Birrell, Minister for Education in the Liberal administration. They told him that they spoke not only on behalf of Mothers' Union members, a considerable number by then, but that they were the voice of an even greater multitude of mothers of the country who would wish their children to be taught, as an integral part of their school curriculum, the faith in which they had themselves been brought up.

The Education Bill was defeated in the House of Lords and Augustine Birrell left Westminster in disgust for a stormy spell in Ireland. Two years later another attempt was made to alter the basis of education. If this had been passed, teaching even in church schools would have been affected but that Bill also foundered. The cause for which the Mothers' Union had fought appeared to have triumphed.

Its leaders were not tempted to feel complacent. The forces of discontent with the established order were strengthening and appeared to be striking at the roots of what they held dear. Even Sunday Schools were being undermined. In the big cities secular Sunday Schools were making their appearance. Working-class children were brought together to learn ideas of revolution. They even sang hymns about a secular society where the workers would be freed from the shackles of Church and State, using the tunes that had been sung by long tradition to Christian words. The Central Council drew up a list of where such subversive Sunday Schools were to be found in the London area and circulated it to all the incumbents, warning them of the dangers.

There were many painful lessons to be learned from the 1914 war. One of them concerned the education of the young men who were dying in their thousands in Flanders mud. Chaplains sent home terrible stories. Many soldiers were pitifully ill-equipped spiritually to face such horrors.

The pressure of the secularist reformers had begun to affect the attitude of churchmen. They admitted that not everything was rosy in the educational work of the Church. Reform there must be. New ideas and methods were essential. But these should develop from the inherited wisdom gained by the Church in teaching the young. They must be kept within the orbit of the Church's life. Those who sought to place education outside any denominational teaching were in danger of throwing away the baby with the bathwater.

In 1917 the Education Committee of the House of Lay-men joined forces with the Mothers' Union to convene a meeting at Church House, Westminster, to demand reform on the right lines. Speakers included Dr Gore, then Bishop of Oxford, the Dean of Canterbury and Mrs Wilberforce who was at that time Central President of the Mothers' Union.

She reiterated the view that 'religion was the root and ground of the whole matter, and not a mere branch of education as some would have us think'. She spoke of the concern mothers felt in the matter. A large gathering of 'working women' in London had recently passed a resolution asking for the Church catechism to be taught in schools.

They felt that the lack of this kind of teaching was causing a lot of trouble among young people.

At its next Central Council meeting the society sent a resolution to the President of the Board of Trade:

'That this meeting of the Central Council of the Mothers' Union welcomes the promise of steps being taken towards securing greater efficiency in general education given by the Minister of Education and desires to urge that, with a view to the upbuilding of character, which is the primary purpose of all true education, there should be included in an early Education Bill provision for the giving of definite religious teaching in all schools and colleges, in accordance with the wishes of parents.'

It was twenty years before a major change was made in the pattern of education. The Mothers' Union kept its members informed of the issues involved in the discussions leading to the 1936 Education Act, particularly stressing the rights of parents who wish their children to be given Church teaching and the need for qualified committed teachers in religious subjects.

When the Act came into force, it altered many things, not always for the better, the Mothers' Union considered. The society took immediate action on the problems it created. In senior schools Church teaching was replaced by an agreed syllabus, drawn up by the various denominations and approved by local education authorities. For the first time, children were taken from church schools when they reached the age of eleven and were educated under the state system. With the vast majority of children being taught in this way, the influence of their homes became even more important. The Mothers' Union renewed its call to parents to be vigilant about the teaching their children were receiving in the things that mattered most. Section 131 of the Act allowed for children in state elementary schools to be withdrawn from religious instruction for teaching by approved sources from their own Churches at the request of the parents.

Because this provision might pass Church parents by unnoticed, the Mothers' Union set about making it known through the wide spread of its membership.

The Second World War with its upheaval of accepted patterns of behaviour once more brought education into public discussion. In 1942 the Mothers' Union was again sharing a public platform at a meeting concerned with the quality of religious instruction in church schools. This time it was allied with the Union of Catholic Mothers and the Free Church Women's Council. All agreed on the need for the best possible teaching within the framework of an agreed syllabus by the best possible people. The Union of Catholic Mothers joined the Mothers' Union in stressing that parents who wished should be granted the right for their children to receive denominational instruction.

By and large the 1944 Education Act was satisfactory from the society's point of view. An agreed syllabus was to be enforced. For the first time every school day must begin with an act of worship. Under this Act parents of children at church schools, like those at state schools, had to opt for denominational instruction. They could not assume that it would be given automatically. Again the Mothers' Union used its influence to make this fact known to parents who might otherwise have not realised that they must take active steps to secure for their children instruction in the faith and practice of the Church of England.

In these last years schools have undergone a not-so-silent revolution. New teaching methods have appeared. The comprehensive system has become the centre of bitter controversy with deeply held feelings on both sides. The Mothers' Union today is a reflection of the whole range of opinions held in society. Some members are chiefly fearful of the loss that new developments might mean. Others welcome them eagerly. Many members these days not only send their children to all kinds of schools but they take up teaching posts themselves. It is not so easy to define a

Mothers' Union line on education as it was in earlier years.

Two issues still unite members. They feel a concern for the preservation of the highest moral standards in all schools and for the rights of church parents to have their children taught according to their beliefs.

Lately the Mothers' Union has provided a valuable meeting-place for parents and teachers who share anxiety about the increasing rejection by older children of society's accepted standards of behaviour. One diocese in Greater London invited to the Mary Sumner House girls nearing the end of their schooldays to discuss problems of relationships, sexual and other, with members of the Mothers' Union who could represent to them the point of view of their parents. Some of their teachers came to hear of the occasion and suggested that it might be mutually beneficial if they met with Mothers' Union members to share their individual insights on these matters. The parents seem to have been told a few home truths. They heard of young people who were given as much as £4 a week to spend on themselves. 'They feel more adult than in fact they are,' a headmaster said. It was a representative father who said that young people going through a difficult stage need to feel that their teachers are on their side. 'Sometimes the parents are not.'

Mothers and their children have changed in many ways since Mary Sumner founded the Mothers' Union. Motherhood has improved in status as psychologists have appeared who insist on the importance of the first few years of a child's life in the formation of its character. There was little help for young mothers a hundred years ago. Now they are bombarded with good advice from all sides. The work of the Mothers' Union has become concentrated on the need for parents to pay as much attention to their children's moral and spiritual development as they do to their physical and mental growth.

What has happened to the adolescent would have startled the early members of the society. Young people have demanded freedom from parental restraints at an ever earlier age. They move into an apparently alien culture of their own, bewildering and even antagonising their parents. The Mothers' Union is caught up in the general maelstrom. Its members' commitment to their responsibility for their children's training is now set against this more difficult background.

Within the traditional structures of the Church, the Mothers' Union continues to explore how parents can help to incorporate the next generation into the Body of Christ. One diocese recently drew together some of its members with clergy and laymen concerned in religious education to take counsel about the meaning of confirmation for young people. Who should be confirmed? Who should do the teaching? Were the real needs of the candidates being satisfied? What part should the family play in the process? A remark by the diocesan secretary shows that, in spite of the difficulties in its path, the work of the Mothers' Union still goes on. 'We had a better idea of working together towards a fuller understanding of Christian education.'

5

FELLOWSHIP IN PRAYER

'The great reserve force'

ONE residentiary canon of an Anglican cathedral calls the diocesan festival of the Mothers' Union an annual miracle. Police usher coaches and private cars to special parking areas. Old hands arrive hours early, well aware that, as every seat will be taken, latecomers will find themselves with a great stone pillar blocking their view. Sometimes the demand is so great that two or even three services have to be arranged.

The cathedral comes alive with a happy buzz. As the hour approaches, movement dies down. There is an expectant silence. The organ surges into life and the processional hymn begins.

It has to be a long hymn. There are well over a hundred banners in the procession. The diocesan banner leads, at first moving disembodied down the side aisle. Then the long file of banners brought from every parish church in the diocese. The embroidery on some representing the Madonna and Child is somewhat faded. Others are almost garishly new, abstract designs perhaps. Each one is recognised by its family among the congregation. Even the most hardened critic of tranditional shibboleths (and there are always some in any Mothers' Union gathering) cannot resist a stirring of pride at seeing her banner in its due place winding through ancient stone arches or Victorian brick. Cathedral clergy receive the banners before the High Altar and stack them in a colourful heap round the sanctuary walls. The service begins.

Let us pray, a distant voice intones and here is the

42

real miracle. All that great assembly of women really prays. The Mothers' Union is remembering that it is committed to the practice of prayer.

What became known as the Third Object was set down by Mary Sumner in Old Alresford. Many members since have.considered it the most significant work of the society. 'To organise in every place a band of Mothers who will unite in prayer, and seek by their own example to lead their families in purity and holiness of life.'

This was Mary Sumner's answer to those who suggested that there were enough societies and meetings of one sort and another already in existence without starting a Mothers' Union. 'The Mothers' Union has a special object in view, which is to raise the moral and religious life of the country through the homes. Union is strength, and if there is a special power in such a Union to gather up the great reserve force of "Mothers' influence", no argument should deter us from joining the Society.'

The prayer she wrote for her new union in Old Alresford underlined the priority of fellowship. 'Unite us together in love and prayer.'

Not that Mothers' Union members, frail humans as they are, have been always at one in perfect charity and un-blemished sanctity, but they have never been allowed to forget that mutual love of God and of each other is of first importance. Every now and then it has seemed that commit-ment to this main purpose was growing dim. Members have been recalled to the practice of regular prayer, essential for those who are pledged to bring all families to a deeper under-standing of the true nature of marriage and family life.

So when the Mothers' Union was facing the reconstruc-tion necessary after the 1914 war, its leaders launched a Peace Campaign of Prayer, calling on members to deepen their own spiritual lives and to help in making homes more worthy of those who laid down their lives to defend them by filling them with the love and knowledge of God. The

Watchword was 'God in the Home'. Every branch was asked to make some special evangelistic effort in its own district. Leaders of each diocese came together for a residential retreat or, at the least, a Quiet Day. This preparation through corporate silence and prayer has continued to be a regular feature in Mothers' Union undertakings. Through it many women have been introduced to deeper levels of prayer and understanding of the scriptures.

During this campaign special times for prayer were kept daily in all the churches, with regular services of Holy Communion. Prayers in many places were linked together by weekly sessions at the Mary Sumner House, then in its temporary quarters in Dean's Yard.

The 1920s were busy years for the Mothers' Union. The world of which it was part seemed to grow ever more hostile to the causes it held dear. By 1933 the Central Council, sensing a cooling of spiritual fires, called all members to a renewal of their personal commitment. The pattern was fundamentally the same as before, preparation in prayer in each diocese, teaching on the true nature of membership in the branches, central acts of witness and dedication. During this Call to Renewal, the waiters in a London hotel near the Mary Sumner House served breakfast to three hundred women who were wrapped in holy silence. Whatever's wrong, they wanted to know. At a final act of corporate witness in the Royal Albert Hall, a great cross rose from banks of flowers in the centre of the stage. The Archbishop of Canterbury charged each member to see always in her home the reality of heaven all about her.

When a second world war brought disruption of settled home life, two diocesan presidents sought the help of the whole movement in tackling a common problem. During the war years many of their members had drifted away from their understanding of what their membership really meant. The call went out to every member in 1946 to re-dedicate and re-affirm the promises she had made when she joined the society. Literature was produced and speakers trained to make clear to every branch the demands of membership. A few withdrew. Most stayed to take part in services on Lady Day that year when each re-affirmed the promises she had taken. Queen Elizabeth, now the Queen Mother, attended a representative gathering in Westminster Abbey symbolising the re-dedication of the whole movement to its ideals.

1956 was the Mothers' Union's eightieth birthday. Celebrations took the form of a call to prayer. One diocese in the north of England made a pilgrimage to York. 'We went by coaches and special trains and women police were imported from other towns to cope with the traffic.

'The numbers were too great even for York Minster to hold and so, by kind permission of the Dean and Chapter, two special services were held for us during the afternoon. It was an amazing sight to watch the first congregation leaving the Minster by the South Door while the second 2,000 women began to pour in at the West Door.'

These big occasions are significant only insofar as they gather up and stimulate the hidden life of steady prayer of the individuals who make up the great throngs. The Mothers' Union has always been concerned with the quality of its members' lives, considering the witness of the whole is only made effective by the contribution of each. The society cannot do their praying for them but it can make expert help available. Priests and lay people who are students of prayer and the scriptures are invited to share their knowledge at the centre, in the dioceses and in each branch.

One of the problems constantly facing the society in this field of communication is the variety of the audience which it is trying to reach, ranging from university graduates to those who find reading a book almost impossible. Churchmanship too varies from the 'higher than Rome' to the rigorously evangelical. Though the age range has tended to be increasingly overweighted on the high side, there are always some very young wives and mothers whose outlook differs sharply from that of their mothers and grandmothers.

The solution has been to provide as great a variety in its teaching on matters spiritual as possible. In 1950 the *Official Workers' Paper* (which later became the *Mothers' Union News*) carried an article designed to be read aloud to a branch in the absence of a speaker.

'But how are we to get to know God? Take a very simple illustration. We know a great deal about our Queen. We know that she is the patron of the Mothers' Union and a member of the Bible Reading Fellowship, that she brought up her children in a Christian way, and that she has a most gracious and friendly smile. All these things and many others, we know *about* her. But suppose, for the sake of argument, the Queen was to come to our Mothers' Union Meeting this afternoon and go round and chat to each one of us—wouldn't we be able to say afterwards, that we not only knew *about* the Queen but that we actually *knew* her? It would make all the difference!

'Lots of people know things *about* God—that He is the Maker of the universe, that He sent His Son, Jesus, to show us what God is like, that He gives the Holy Spirit at Baptism and Confirmation, and many other things they know *about* God. But how many really *know* Him in the other sense?'

The following year 'educated women' for whom *Mothers in Council* was designed were reading of a God who was difficult to know, *Deus Absconditus*, in a sermon by Dr A. R. Vidler. 'And turn now to Jesus Christ. Is it not claimed that He came to bring light amid all this darkness, to resolve all these enigmas, to put doubt to death? Evidently, however, He has not done so. And, in fact, so far from the claim that Jesus is the revealer or the revelation of God clearing up all enigmas, it might be truer to say that it *gathers* them up, focusses and intensifies them.'

All have found special value in one member sharing her experiences with her fellows. A woman who lost her husband in the First World War and her son in the second tells what it has meant to her. 'Another thing to remember is that people are sometimes inclined to avoid the bereaved, so that if we want to make and keep friends we must hide our grief, and never show the pangs we feel when *their* sons come home. We must learn to be in the company of proud grannies, too, and never betray the longing for those dream grandchildren we shall now never have the joy of holding in our arms.'

When a visiting lecturer addressed a speakers' conference in Oxford, he might have been summing up what the Mothers' Union has set itself to do in its teaching work. 'We have to view the truth through present-day eyes, bringing out of our treasure things new and old, interpreting afresh in every age the everlasting Gospel.'

In 1921 a valuable aspect of the Mothers' Union work of intercession was started when the wife of a parish priest sent a scheme of prayer to the Mary Sumner House. As an invalid she had not been able to take an active part in affairs but had been strengthened in facing her own problems by regular interceding for others. The idea was welcomed by others in similar circumstances. An Invalid Members' Prayer Circle was formed which drew in those who were house-bound through illness or age. It functioned faithfully until 1971 when it continued under a new name, the Indoor Members' Prayer Circle. A paper is circulated three times a year to members giving particular subjects for prayer and thanksgiving.

Those responsible for this work are anxious that it should not be seen as a poor relation. As one report of its Central Correspondent said: 'Correspondents have asked me to make it clear that Members of the Prayer Circle are not by any means all old, nor are they poor and illiterate. One Diocesan Correspondent tells me that among her Members are two ex-Presiding Members, four ex-Enrolling Members, and many educated women of all classes. Of course there are many poor and old Members whom we try to help, and for whose sake we keep the Intercessions as simple as possible, but there have never been any complaints that the Intercessions are too simple for anyone.' This same account mentions the death of a blind member who 'had the joy of the intercessions in Braille', thanks to the efforts of a sighted member.

Another body linked through prayer was started in 1905 when the Mothers' Union launched special work among nurses who ministered to families and could do a great deal to encourage mothers to accept the teaching of the Mothers' Union. They not only valued membership of the Nurses' Fellowship for themselves but were instrumental in starting branches among the women in their care. Their regular bulletins kept them informed of the work of the society. Prayers were drawn up for their own use and for them to use with those who are ill. Membership has been specially helpful to nurses working overseas, often remote from colleagues with similar interests.

During the last twenty years more than two hundred members with sons who are Anglican priests have been linked with Roman Catholic women through the Union des Mamans de Prêtres et de Religieux. When one of these mothers attended their anniversary party in Belgium, she found herself feted with champagne and warmly embraced by Madame Mathieu who sounds a veritable Mary Sumner of a rather different tradition.

Over the last fifty years the Wave of Prayer has swept on continuously through the Mothers' Union. Every diocese is remembered in turn, being allotted a few days each year. Month by month the schedule is printed in the society's journals. To take an extract at random: 'April 1–5. Iran, The Sudan, Rwanda: Ely.'

Some members give a few moments' thought at some point of each day to the places to be held in special remembrance. One woman, seeing on television news an account of flooding somewhere in the world is likely to exclaim, 'That's sometime in February.' When the time comes round for a diocese to be remembered, its branches are expected to make particular efforts in prayer for the work of the whole. Times are allotted to various churches so that a continuous watch is kept throughout the world on behalf of homes and families.

The joining together of dioceses on certain days was originally the result of a rule of thumb division of the year. It has meant that close links have been forged between members in different parts of the world. An English diocese studies the background of 'our linked diocese'. Letters are exchanged between members and sometimes visits are made possible, often through funds raised by special branch and deanery efforts.

The Wave of Prayer has proved invaluable in bringing alive to each member the general exhortation that they should pray for each other. Half-a-million women is something difficult to imagine. But when these women's names can be listed and their homes visualised, the process comes to life.

Some members have also taken on a special responsibility for praying for the work of the Mothers' Union as a whole. A quarterly paper informs them of conferences and business meetings which they can hold in their hearts while they are busy on their own affairs.

Out of the various calls to the members to be more faithful in the work of prayer, some have been drawn together here and there to meet as a group month by month, sometimes week by week. From 1946 prayer groups have become a regular part of many branches. Their hope is not that an élite of particularly pious souls should be created but that their quiet influence would permeate for good the life of the whole.

A member of a branch where the work of prayer is given its due priority once set out the fruits of its labours. Members become more friendly to each other and help in each other's difficulties. They are not a closed circle but are helped to see more clearly needs beyond the branch. They are eager to build up the life of their Church. They know the power of prayer and become as individuals ever more serene and joyful. They are trying to find God's will and to be obedient to it.

Most branches would admit that they fall short of their high calling but many have gone on trying over the years. Such achievements are hard to assess in words. A layman, talking to an assembled conference of diocesan workers, gave them a prayer he found helpful himself. It could be a motto for the whole Mothers' Union, bound together in a common witness of prayer.

'O Secret Christ, Lord of the Rose of Dawn, hide me within Thy silent peace, that throughout the turmoil of the day, I may abide within the quiet of the daybreak.'

6

MARRIAGE MATTERS

'The solemn bond of matrimony'

THE second and third of the original Central Objects of the Mothers' Union, to help mothers to a sense of responsibility for their children's training and to organise a fellowship of prayer, have called forth sympathy and admiration from Church people and from many who would not profess to be Christians. The first Object on the other hand has led to constant heart-searching within the ranks of the society and widespread criticism from without.

It appears in the 1926 Constitution as: 'To Uphold the Sanctity of Marriage' and carries a footnote: 'In the words "to uphold the Sanctity of Marriage" the Mothers' Union affirms the Christian principle of the permanence of the relationship between husband and wife.' Few phrases outside holy writ have been subjected to closer scrutiny. Their history has been brooded over, especially the fact that they did not appear with Mary Sumner's original two objects. Did this mean that the Mothers' Union added the idea of indissoluble marriage to its original marching orders? If this could be proved, it might be easier to shake off what some have seen as an intolerable burden in twentieth-century conditions.

There is indisputable evidence that Mary Sumner from the first days of the society held the definite view that divorce should not be made easier. In 1892 she wrote in the *Mothers' Union Journal*: 'Our readers will see that a third Object has been added to the Mothers' Union aims. It has been placed first—"To uphold the Sanctity of Marriage"—

because marriage lies at the very foundation of family life,
and because it is felt that more attention should be paid to
the solemnity and duties and responsibilities of holy marriage.
It is declared in God's word to be a type or shadow of the
spiritual union which is between Christ and His Church.
Does this not sanctify and elevate the solemn bond of
marriage and make it a very sacred and heavenly thing? . . .
Sad to say, terrible evils are now advocated which tend to
lower, to sap and destroy the very foundation of home-life.
There are men and women who deny the life-long union, the
religious bond of holy matrimony, and desire that it should
be a mere contract, to end when either party grows tired
of the other, or when there is unkindness, and quarrelling
and incompatibility of temper or the like. . . . Christ has
taught us what marriage and home should be. His words are
plain concerning the absolute oneness of holy marriage:
"for this cause shall a man leave his father and mother and
cleave to his wife". "What therefore God hath joined together
let not man put asunder." '

Opinion in the Church against wider divorce facilities had
been brought into conflict with the State some years before
the Mothers' Union was founded. In 1857 the first Divorce
Law had been passed which took legislation on marriage
cases out of the hands of ecclesiastical authorities. Many
Church leaders had spoken out about the dangers inherent
in a situation where marriages could be dissolved at the
judgement of secular courts though their attitude to indissolubility was not so uniform at that time as it became in
the first half of the twentieth century.

Joyce Coombs in her valuable study of George and Mary
Sumner has shown conclusively that Mary Sumner, through
her family connections, must have been well aware of the
issues at stake in 1857. As the women's organisation which
she had founded grew to become a force to be reckoned with,
she put it behind whole-hearted opposition to any move to
make divorce easier to obtain. She had the members'

complete support in those years. In 1898 a diocese was petitioning Central Council for the First Object to be extended to include the indissolubility as well as the sanctity of marriage. It was not easy to change the wording of a constitution so recently established in law but the Central Council were at pains to explain publicly that the sanctity of marriage implied the concept of indissolubility.

In 1923, when the society was again under pressure, it re-stated its position on marriage as 'a life-long and indissoluble union of one man with one woman to the exclusion of all others on either side'. Great care was taken when the 1926 Constitution was framed to leave no shadow of doubt. The Mothers' Union was pledged to work in all possible ways to preserve marriage as a relationship that cannot be broken except by death.

This work was seen as having two inter-relating spheres. The whole society could be united in public action when the cause of life-long marriage appeared to be under attack. Each member in her own life, using her personal influence in her family and community, was expected to bear witness to the belief that marriage was part of God's plan for mankind and must be regulated by New Testament teaching as set out in the Service of Holy Matrimony in the Book of Common Prayer.

To implement this witness of personal commitment by each member, it seemed essential as the society developed to lay down rules which excluded some women from membership. Those who had themselves been a party to divorce proceedings would weaken the stand of the whole. Their exclusion from the full fellowship of the society was necessary if it was to witness to what it held to be the truth. Critics who found themselves out of sympathy with the Mothers' Union position on marriage were quick to point to regulations excluding divorced women or those who had married a divorced man as uncharitable and contrary to the spirit of a society pledged to the building of up fellowship.

Meanwhile the Mothers' Union tried hard to interpret its support of the sanctity of marriage in positive ways. It set about teaching the women with whom it was in touch the nature of Christian marriage and its implications for those who embarked on it. Again the instruction has been given in a variety of settings and wide educational levels. Experts on marriage lecture and write, from theologians to anthropologists, sociologists and psychiatrists. Outline talks are drawn up for those speaking to branch meetings. Books are recommended for study. Pamphlets are produced.

The position of the society as a whole that emerges from this mass of teaching material has remained unchanged over the years of its existence. Its view of marriage is not, it maintains, something thought up by the Mothers' Union and imposed on its members. It is that given to his followers by the Lord Jesus Christ. It is clearly expressed in the Anglican marriage service used in every parish church.

While it might be tempting to take the view that Christian marriage is different in essence from marriage among those who do not believe in the Christian gospel, the Mothers' Union, in accordance with what it considers to be the teaching of its Church, has always maintained that this is not possible. Though the practising Christian has access to spiritual strength through the sacraments of grace to uphold him in difficulties and problems as they occur, all marriage, however undertaken, is part of the pattern of behaviour ordained by God for all mankind.

The most primitive communities demonstrate the need for society to order the way men and women live together. The well-being of children demands a stable and enduring family background. The study of history underlines the dangers to society of allowing the life-long nature of the marriage relationship to become eroded.

Against current trends, the Mothers' Union continued to maintain that chastity is still possible and essential, both within marriage and outside it. Sexual experience cannot be separated from ongoing responsibility for the other partner and from the children that might result. There is, it felt, a danger in too easy an acceptance of romantic attitudes to love. Marriage should be entered upon with care and dedication. Love that is to last for life and provide the necessary setting for children to grow up in is more concerned with giving than with taking. It is tested and refined by adversity which is bound to come in some measure to every family. There can be no term set on the forgiveness one human being extends to another. Even seventy times seven is not enough.

Against this background the Mothers' Union upheld the view that it is not possible to break a marriage by decree of man, however desirable it might occasionally seem. The undertaking of a marriage creates a relationship between two people which cannot be wiped out. A man and woman stay husband and wife as inescapably as a father remains father to his son however much either might wish it could be otherwise.

It is easy to see how these principles could alienate those who were facing acute distress in their marriages. However widespread divorce has become, the breakdown of marriage is a painful experience for those involved. At a time when they are in need of support and are often wrestling with deep feelings of guilt, an agency of the Church appears to condemn them by its uncompromising attitude.

It is not easy to assess the positive results that have emerged from years of Mothers' Union teaching. Those who move round its branches meet here and there with women whose marriages have passed through tribulation to such an extent that, but for the understanding and strengthening they found in their membership, they would have had recourse to the divorce courts. They find instead that they have won through to a greater happiness in their marriages than they had ever known before.

Such experiences are naturally not talked about much in

public. An anonymous member raised a rare voice in a copy of *Mothers' Union News*. 'I joined the Mothers' Union because my marriage was in a mess,' she wrote. During the 1945 war, her husband was sent overseas and she found herself moving into a new life. The home she made for her daughter and herself was so satisfying that she began to hope he would not come back. She was just about ready to fall in love with another man, but at this point the vicar's wife suggested she join the Mothers' Union in the village. She refused, considering its First Object narrow-minded. Yet this invitation made her examine her attitude to her absent husband. She began to be plagued with guilt which was only resolved when she made herself confide in the vicar who main reaction was that she should stop thinking so much about herself. She was soon admitted to the Mothers' Union.

'My husband came home and we settled down to a marriage enriched by the knowledge of what we had so nearly lost. Our daughter is married with a family of her own, and it was only quite recently that I discovered how terrified she had been that something unknown but dreadful, was threatening our family happiness at the time of which I have been telling you.'

Though the Mothers' Union has preserved the appearance of unanimity in its defence of life-long marriage in public, it has been subject to many tensions within its own ranks on the matter. This has not implied any weakening in its beliefs about the nature of marriage. The questioning has come from workers in parishes who have to administer the regulations barring some women, among them those who are regular communicants. The society has been constantly challenged to assess its position on membership.

As more and more families were affected by marriage breakdown, the Mothers' Union became increasingly conscious of the need of support and help for the divorced. When in 1959 the Company of Compassion was set up to help men and women faced with problems of loneliness and

with heavy responsibilities as the result of the breakdown of
their marriages, it was fully supported by the Mothers'
Union. Its members were invited to attend the society's
meetings and activities. Regular information was given so
that, when Mothers' Union members met people needing its
help, they could be referred to the local organisation of the
Company of Compassion.

There has never been any difference of opinion in the
Mothers' Union about its responsibility for upholding the
sanctity of marriage to those concerned with the country's
legislation. Under the 1857 Divorce Act, a Divorce Court
was established, removing marriage cases from the jurisdiction of church authorities. Adultery was then the only
ground permitted in pleas for the dissolution of marriage.
If a wife was pleading the case, she had to prove also such
aggravating circumstances as extreme cruelty. It cost a great
deal of money to obtain such decrees. Those championing
the rights of the poor set about making the obtaining of
divorce available to all who wished for it, whatever their
financial circumstances.

To Mary Sumner the 1857 Divorce Act had been an
unmitigated disaster. But if it could not be undone, at least
the damage it had caused ought not to be extended. The
suggestion being made was that divorce jurisdiction should
be given to county courts. She alerted the Mothers' Union
members to the dangers of these proposals and set them to
the task of resisting them in all possible ways.

The Central Council protested 'in the strongest manner'
against any multiplication of divorce courts, sending a copy
of its resolution to every member of the House of Lords. It
coupled with this its objection to the widespread reporting
of details of divorce proceedings which it considered made
unwholesome reading for decent families.

As the agitation grew for more divorce facilities, Parliament was forced to take some action. A Royal Commission
on Divorce and Matrimonial Causes was set up. The

Mothers' Union set about preparing its evidence. Church leaders known to be active in opposition were consulted. Diocesan leaders were charged with bringing the issues involved to every member in the branches. 31,000 'educated women' and 85,000 'working mothers' signed protest forms to be presented to the Commission.

By the time a Mothers' Union delegation appeared before the Commission in person, Mary Sumner, now over eighty, had resigned from the leadership. Lady Chichester who succeeded her as Central President went with two other members to give evidence. None of the three had been brought up to expect that they would ever be faced with such a public ordeal.

The majority of the Royal Commission members subsequently reported that divorce should be extended in certain cases. A minority who could not agree signed a separate report. From their evidence it is clear that the statements which described the Mothers' Union position had played a large part in their thinking. They considered it as specially valuable as little had been heard otherwise from the point of view of the 'respectable working classes'. The signatories of this minority report turned to the Mothers' Union to make their position widely known. It was a job in which the society already had a great deal of experience.

In 1917 a Matrimonial Causes Bill made its appearance in the House of Commons; the Mothers' Union was determined to oppose it root and branch. It looked round for allies. A room in the Dean's Yard Mary Sumner House was earmarked as headquarters of a Marriage Defence Council which the society set up in conjunction with several other church bodies, the Women's Movement and the Labour Party. Mothers' Union branches organised petitions against the Bill and each sent them to its Member of Parliament.

The legislation foundered but the groundswell for reform continued until 1937 when Mr A. P. Herbert, as he was then, got his Marriage Bill on to the statute book. The Mothers'

Union had fought hard against its provisions for extending the grounds of divorce. It felt particularly strongly about the clause which could result in a wife being granted more money if she was divorced than if she applied for a judicial separation. Separation, the society felt, was to be preferred to divorce in cases of hardship as it left the door open for reconciliation.

The result of the 1937 Act was, as the Mothers' Union had prophesied, that divorce came to be accepted as the usual way out of a marriage that was proving unsatisfactory. Circumstances of parties to divorce petitions were increasingly manipulated to come within the existing grounds for divorce until the law was in danger of falling into contempt. Individual Members of Parliament put pressure on the government to overhaul the whole field of divorce legislation. In 1951 another Royal Commission was appointed. This time its powers were widened to include 'the need to promote healthy and happy married life and to safeguard the interests and well-being of children'.

The Memorandum submitted to it by the Mothers' Union was an informed and careful document. It pleaded for clarification of the true nature of marriage which, it maintained, was the same whether vows were taken in church or before a registrar. It spelled out the effects of divorce on the family life of the country. It pressed for careful thought to be given to judicial separation and nullity in any new marriage legislation. It stressed the need for reconciliation facilities to be made available before divorce was granted. It considered that the welfare of any children should be of prime importance in pleas for the dissolution of marriage.

This time the Central President to appear before the Commission was Mrs Basil Roberts who was accompanied by three other Mothers' Union members. The Report when it appeared was too inconclusive to prompt immediate legislation. The Commission had come into being as the result of a Private Member's Bill which sought to add marriage breakdown as a cause for divorce, thus removing the need to prove before the courts that the 'guilty party' had committed a matrimonial offence. The members of the Royal Commission turned out to be almost equally divided on the advisability of this fundamentally new attitude to divorce so for the time being the matter rested.

The Divorce Law Reform Society continued to campaign for the law to be changed to include the concept of marriage breakdown. The Mothers' Union continued to oppose it. The Press reported the clash of views, and spokesmen for both sides were interviewed before television cameras.

When Mr Leo Abse introduced a Matrimonial Clauses and Reconciliation Bill, the Mothers' Union protested forcibly against the clause that a decree of divorce should be granted after seven years' separation at the petition of either spouse. This would have meant that people could have been divorced against their wishes. Mothers' Union members were among those who might suffer under such a provision. As it became obvious that the difference of opinion over this clause might result in the whole Bill foundering, it was withdrawn at the third reading. The resultant Act contained much that the Mothers' Union welcomed, specially the improved facilities for reconciliation in marriages that were running into difficulties.

Dissatisfaction with the law as it stood continued. In 1969 a Divorce Reform Bill made its appearance. The Mothers' Union was instrumental in drawing together women's organisations to demand that fuller consideration should be given to those families left unprovided for after a divorce had been granted. The Bill had talked of 'the best arrangement that can be made in the circumstances' and this, it was felt, might be interpreted as being very little. Some improvements were made in the committee stages for providing for any children in a divorce.

The new principle of irretrievable breakdown of marriage being a cause for divorce appeared again. This time five years' desertion was suggested as the period after which divorce could be granted at the request of either party. The Mothers' Union protested to Members of Parliament and was widely quoted by the Press which had labelled the proposed legislation a Casanova's charter.

Mrs Joanne Hallifax, Central President of the Mothers' Union, together with leading members of the National Board of Catholic Women, the Medical Womens' Federation and the Council of Married Women, signed the following resolution:

'We believe that this Clause, which introduces divorce by compulsion after five years' desertion by the petitioner weighs the scales heavily against those who have done no more than maintain their marriage rights and, for the first time in English Law, it allows a defaulter to benefit from wrong doing. In addition it could over-ride the respondent's religious and conscientious objections.'

This time the Bill went through and the new basis for divorce was introduced into the courts. To the Mothers' Union in particular it meant that those who maintained that their marriage was life-long were no longer necessarily supported by the laws of their country. It is as yet too early for its effects on family life to be assessed.

It might be concluded that now the laws of marriage and divorce have been changed so fundamentally the work of the Mothers' Union has been in vain. All the long hard years of study and discussion, meetings and resolutions, prayers and concern have had no more effect than a man trying to hold back the onward surge of an incoming tide. Yet the Mothers' Union had no choice but to act as it did. The truth it saw was no less true because it became increasingly unpopular. Whatever the outcome in legislative terms, its witness to the life-long nature of marriage was a necessary feature in the whole picture. The Mothers' Union spoke clearly and faithfully for Christian families who were part of the community for which laws were being framed.

Because it was constantly forced into opposition and was always under fire, the presentation of its beliefs had to be sharp and clear. There are few church people of any sort and gender who are so knowledgeable on matters of faith as Mothers' Union members are on the Christian doctrine of marriage. Its supporters, and there have been many, were not always as widely reported as its detractors but their understanding of what the Mothers' Union was trying to do came all the sweeter. They helped to remind the world at large that the society's attitudes were not always negatively in opposition. There was a positive side to its work.

1963 was an example of this. Christian Family Year provided a chance for the society to develop and intensify its service to all families in the many communities in which it was at work. One of the main features of the year was thanksgiving for the many marriages that have brought great happiness to the parties to them, to their families and to those who come in contact with them. These are often the forgotten multitude as laws and social services concentrate on the comparative few that come to grief.

The Mothers' Union held one of its big services, this time in St Paul's Cathedral in London, when husbands and wives rendered thanks for their own marriages and re-affirmed the vows they had taken when they started on them. The Queen and Prince Philip stood together at the head of the congregation. Prince Philip read the story of the wedding at Cana of Galilee. A member who was present with her husband said, 'These were simply two out of hundreds of married people, all members of one congregation, and all remembering, in the presence of God and of each other, the God-given blessings of marriage and of family life'.

7

GOING ABROAD

'My dear daughters'

ONE day in 1900 Mary Sumner, now a matronly white-haired lady, took up her pen in the room overlooking the quiet Winchester garden. 'My dear daughters' she began, and ended 'Your loving white mother'. The latest members of the Mothers' Union had just taken their promises in Madagascar. Mary Sumner was delighted with them. 'Do you know', she said to a missionary she met, 'that I have five hundred dear black daughters in Madagascar?' Their attitude to her was one of loving reverence. 'We thank you very, very much for the beautiful members' cards, we, your children in the Lord.'

Up to the present day the memory of Mary Sumner is kept green in many parts of the world. A boat in which a worker visits branches in Bangladesh is called, in Bengali lettering, *Mary Sumner*. West African members who raised money to build their own headquarters called them The Mary Sumner House. The life of Mary Sumner is serialised on a radio programme in Tristan da Cunha. When thousands gathered at a cathedral in Uganda to celebrate fifty years of Mothers' Union presence in their country, they sang a hymn to the tune of Good King Wenceslas:

> Let us begin by thanking
>   Mary Sumner,
> Our Founder, who began slowly
>   with a few people.
> Now it has spread everywhere.
>   Let us thank Sumner.

Mothers' Union literature first went overseas in the
luggage of army wives. Some whose husbands were stationed
at Aldershot had attended a meeting of the new society in
1888. By the following year when they were sent to India,
they set about launching the Mothers' Union there.

It began to spread at the same astonishing rate as at
home. Branches on Gibraltar and Malta fired women who
subsequently moved on to start branches in other parts of
the world. Soon the work was increasing apace in army bases
in India, Burma and Egypt. From then onwards wives of
service men have found membership particularly valuable
when they are moved to strange places. Kindred spirits are
waiting to welcome them into a familiar fellowship.

At the RAF station in Singapore during the 1960s, for
example, the Mothers' Union branch reported that members
constantly visited new families moving in, offering friendship and local information. Their meetings were held in the
mornings while it was still comparatively cool. Their
leaders were destined to see few of the fruits of their labours.
As soon as women were integrated into the branch, many
would move on to other postings where, it was hoped, they
would become useful members of another Mothers' Union.

Not all the first branches overseas were planted by army
wives. One of the earliest was in Ontario. A clergyman's
widow went back to visit her childhood home in the Winchester area. When she returned to Canada, she had caught
the Mothers' Union infection. The list of new branches
started overseas soon read like the index to an atlas. Adelaide,
Jamaica, Nagasaki, New South Wales, Shanghai. The
British were on the move all round their extensive possessions.
The Mothers' Union soon collected an enthusiastic army of
emissaries.

At first Africa was slower off the mark though it was later
to become the true heart-land of the Mothers' Union. South
Africa was very much in the mind of British people during
the Boer War. In 1902 Mary Sumner reported to the Central

Council: 'In several parts of our South African Colonies there are Members who are eager to start work as soon as the state of the country allows of any definite organisation being set on foot. It is felt to be of the greatest importance to the future of the Colony that the home life of our fellow countrymen should be based on the principles which guide the Mothers' Union.'

Two experienced leaders were sent to South Africa to help start the work on a sound basis, financed by gifts from English members. They were the first of a long line of workers overseas. Their efforts proved successful. African and coloured women sought membership eagerly and have remained among the society's most enthusiastic supporters.

By 1904 Mary Sumner was telling the Central Council that 'the Mothers' Union had gained a firm foothold in nearly every British Colony and that it was warmly appreciated'. The work of translating the society's literature had started. The Central Fund, for example, made a grant of £20 to translate literature into Hindustani. Money was made available for workers in various parts of the world. £20 a year was considered sufficient to enable an Indian diocese to support a full-time organiser. The missionary societies began to value the work the Mothers' Union was doing among families in many parts of the world. The Society for the Propagation of the Gospel in 1909 appealed for workers; this began a close partnership between the Mothers' Union and all the Church bodies responsible for work overseas.

When George the Fifth was crowned in 1911, many representatives came to London from his dominions overseas. The Mothers' Union seized the opportunity to gather its supporters together to confer about their particular problems and opportunities. Out of these discussions came the formation of an Overseas Committee which has continued to be responsible for the work outside the home country to the present day.

The ten-yearly gatherings in London of the bishops of the
Anglican Communion for the Lambeth Conferences have
been used by the society to gather together members from
many places for a World-Wide Conference. Many of their
delegates were wives of bishops who were accompanying
their husbands to London.

The Mothers' Union continued to flourish wherever the
Anglican Communion was to be found and in some places
increased mightily. Problems multiplied as teaching on
marriage and family life that had originated in Victorian
England had to be interpreted to women born into a
variety of different cultures and traditions.

A common hazard that has always faced workers overseas
(at the present time there are 120 supported by the Overseas
Fund) is the distances they have to travel in the course of
their work. Their reports to headquarters read like a Pauline
travelogue. Even today a great deal of walking goes on. To
reach the more remote branches workers must undertake
day-long treks. In New Guinea one worker was faced with a
mountain trail which included the crossing of a flimsy cane
bridge suspended above a fast-flowing river. She confessed
that she crossed it many times in her imagination beforehand.

'It was an hour's walk to the cane bridge and every step I
took the bridge got bigger and bigger until I had visions of
something like the Sydney Harbour bridge suspended from
the tree tops across a foaming harbour! It wasn't anything
as bad as we imagined—four strands of cane for our feet and
four strands on either side for rails, a rushing Kamusi River
thirty feet below and a suspension of 200 feet. In bare feet
we felt our way on the plaited cane and clung on to the side
rails with our hands, keeping our eyes straight ahead so as
not to feel giddy by the slight sway of the bridge and the
rushing river below. Half way across I heard a splash and a
shout. It was my cooking pot breaking on the rocks below!'

In Pakistan travel is sometimes by buffalo cart. 'The
buffaloes don't keep to the roads, but go over ploughed

fields, down steep rough paths to cross rivers, and up and down deep ditches at the side of the road, and if one doesn't look intently on what is ahead all the time, one suddenly finds the cart swiftly going down a steep bank and the buffaloes going at a running speed, the cart being at an angle of about 45°!'

Another Mothers' Union worker was wrestling with very different travelling conditions in Korea. The cold was so intense when she arrived at one mountain village that she found a little girl losing toes from frost-bite. She supplied her with socks. Another two children were in urgent need of operations. 'I've put both of them into hospital', she announced, 'even though I have no money to pay the bills. . . . We had one very exciting evening during my stay; at 9 p.m. a girl arrived saying that a man had returned home to his very remote mountain house to find his wife, all alone except for two toddlers, had given birth to a baby boy and died. The baby was alive, but the father had no help. So we left the house in my Mothers' Union car and drove for about half an hour—the windscreen was frozen and visibility was nil. When we reached the mountain track we had to park the car and start climbing, and for two hours crossed frozen rivers on stones on the ice or crawled across wooden bridges less than a foot wide and with no rails, always climbing. It was a full moon, and the track so frozen it was like glass. A good deal of the time we walked on the rough paddy fields risking sprained ankles but at least we stayed on our feet. At last we came to the house and by the light of a tiny oil lamp found the baby boy rolled in filthy rags lying in a corner of the room. We cleaned him with oil and I dressed him in the clean clothes we had brought with us. The father didn't want him so we took him with us on the long walk back to the car, John Lee very bravely carrying him down the icy track. We arrived home at 2.30 a.m., the baby was handed over to a kind Korean mother, and we tumbled into bed, on the floor, of course.'

Africa present workers with all possible hazards, swamps, deserts, mountains, flooded rivers and vast distances. One worker has to travel round an area of 75,000 miles. Extracts from the diary of a Kenya worker would suggest that they must sometimes wonder if their journeys are really necessary.

'I did all the driving which was rather a strain as it was the rainy season and the roads were a mess of mud and water. Fortunately people were very helpful, pushing us through the mud. One place we went to, the women had heard that we were coming the previous day and had waited until 5 p.m. Sending news of meetings out to the country areas is not easy and messages often get lost. At another place most of the women had gone to a funeral, and we only had eight at the meeting.'

Cars supplied by the Overseas Fund are an essential tool in the work. Some of them become personalities treasured by those who spend many hours travelling in them. An ancient Land-Rover was christened Lucy by the worker. She was specially precious as she functioned in Rhodesia and after UDI could not be replaced. 'Whenever Lucy has an attack of old age, she always waits until she has got me safely home to base and then collapses almost outside the front door!' In 1971 a Mothers' Union car in Rhodesia was involved in a tragic accident when two African workers, Lydia Duiker and Ida Damasene, were killed on their way to open a new Mothers' Union group. Both were priests' wives and left large families.

Language is a constant problem in the work. Imparting ideas about the Christian principles of family relationships is hard enough in one's own language. It becomes a formidable task when undertaken through an interpreter. Learning the local language can be easier said than done when a worker is responsible for an area in which several dozen languages are spoken. Even local leaders can find themselves faced with difficulties in communicating.

In the first impetus of starting branches, interpreters had

to be used a great deal as the English ladies took their message to the villages and towns round about. As education developed, often through Church agencies, and English became the lingua franca, things grew easier. In the last few years, language has again become a problem in many places. Newly independent countries encourage the use of local languages. The Mothers' Union is having to come to terms with this situation. In 1966, for example, a training course was held in Nairobi entirely in Swahili for the first time.

Independent countries meant independent Churches with their own clergy managing their own affairs. The Mothers' Union was late to grasp the implications, perhaps because the ties of mutual concern had been forged too strongly to be easily broken, perhaps because much of its work was concerned with the poorest families who needed the help that more affluent countries could provide.

But in the last few years the pattern has been for local women to take increasing responsibility for the work. Leaders are emerging like Martha Ngcukuva who in 1964 was described in a South African journal: 'Despite the high position she had attained, Mrs Ngcukuva never lost touch with ordinary people. Her devotion to the Church and her humble spirit put her on an equality with all with whom she has had to deal both great and small. Under her leadership the Mothers' Union in the Diocese has grown, not only outwardly in numbers, but in the inward understanding of the Christian ideal of womanhood, of which she herself sets so fine an example.'

In 1967 the first African to become bishop of Zululand admitted Rosaline Jali as diocesan president. In Uganda the wife of the Kabaka's private secretary was trained to take over from a European worker. When the bishop in Polynesia grew impatient of waiting in the queue for a worker at the Mary Sumner House in London, he found a worker for himself, Toe'mu Misiele Fineanganofo. Every European official of the Mothers' Union in Melanesia has her Melanesian counterpart preparing to take over full responsibility.

From its beginnings the society has been in touch with many homes in the world where poverty exists on a scale long forgotten in the west. A worker in 1962 gives this account of Jamaican conditions: 'The Mothers' Union is helping to think out the problems confronting Jamaica at the present time—the disparity between the "haves" and the "have-nots", the lack of adequate and proper housing (without which it is so difficult to bring up one's children); the poverty and the misunderstanding, the illegitimacy, the strange sects, the unemployment, and many more.'

Many African societies present the Mothers' Union with special problems. It finds itself teaching about Christian marriage to women who were given to their husbands under local customs. Bride price figures large in these negotiations. In many places a cattle marriage is considered sufficient even among Christians.

In 1966 Nigerian members were deep in study of problems created by their particular brand of inflation: 'One other concern of the M.U. members is the soaring rate of bride price in the country. This high bride price has left many girls hanging without husbands because the men find it difficult to save up for bride price. In some cases this prohibitive bride price has forced many to elope with their lovers, while some marry without any parental blessings. . . . A Committee has been set up in the Diocese comprising M.U. members and men of broad outlook to examine the matter objectively. . . . The M.U. members feel that one way of demonstrating what they preach is to begin with themselves by giving out their daughters without the long cherished method of bleeding their prospective sons-in-law to death.'

Such problems have led Mothers' Union workers to set about teaching girls the real meaning of marriage before they reach marriageable age. In Lebombo a Guild of St

Agnes was formed, affectionately known The Aggies, where girls learned home-making skills while imbibing Christian ideals of marriage and family life.

Polygamy has raised many problems. The Mothers' Union with its insistence on the life-long relationship of one man with one woman has come to be known in some places as the society for women who stay with their husbands.

Yet when traditional tribal ways break down, it is not all gain. A diocesan synod in Tanzania included a good proportion of Mothers' Union members. The Mothers' Union worker is reporting:

'One interesting item on the agenda which affects the responsibilities of women in particular, was the possibility of reviving and bringing into the Christian way of life, some of the old customs which are good and which have been cast off with the bad ones, to the detriment of the life of the community. There is no getting away from the fact that many more unmarried girls are producing babies than ever before, the situation is worsening. Various reasons are given; the fact that girls have so much more freedom these days, that they so often go away from their home influence to school, when very young, that they are able to compete on equal terms with boys and in many cases are thrown into their company a great deal. European type of dances where boys and girls dance together (so alien to African custom) is considered too great an intimacy. But the greatest of all is the fact that the recognised ritual of teaching girls—and boys also—at puberty is no longer practised in many places. Girls go away to school with no teaching whatsoever from their mothers regarding the functions and wonder of their bodies. They are left to find these things out in a secret way among their fellows and so they do not learn to reverence their own bodies or those of others.

'Committees are being formed to think about and discuss these things and the members of the Mothers'

Union have been given the responsibility of seeing that the girls do have teaching—and at the right time.'

One custom still accepted in many African communities has raised practical problems. The older women expect to rule the roost. Some insist on being leaders though they are not the most suitable for the job. They can carry the sense of their own position to the extent of keeping their daughters-in-law out of the Mothers' Union. It needs a great deal of tact to create conditions that will attract the younger women.

The growth of industrial Africa has had grave effects on family life in the villages. Men disappear to jobs in mines and factories for months on end. Some send money home regularly; others drift away from their families. Those who return are different after experience of the city.

'Men coming home from the south bring dress-lengths, pots and pans, a fluency in English and Afrikaans and new ideas, but very few women ever leave home; it is against government policy and against custom. Many have little or no schooling; so they are not only educationally backward, but behind their husbands: "Why can't *you* cook and keep house like people in the south?"

'The idea of a "School for Women", as it became known, was therefore hailed as a means of progress and emancipation. The married women are of an intelligent and independent turn of mind. When a new idea such as of women's meetings is put to them, they will immediately seize on the crucial points. "We will need training, won't we?" "If we tell them about Christian marriage many women will bring their problems to us—what do we do then?" "How can we keep flies away when we live in unprotected kraals?" As well as learning new things it means being linked with other women—"We did not know so many other people were thinking of us", they said in one place, on hearing of the world-wide Mothers' Union.'

The society has to tackle family problems in expanding African towns also. In East Africa the Diocesan President tells of work being undertaken: 'These groups have within them Anglicans, Lutherans, Menonites, a few Roman Catholics and a few Moslems. We also have an occasional second wife! We welcome any who turn up or are brought along by their friends, as we are glad of the opportunity to tell them what the Christian Gospel is all about, and what is characteristic of a Christian home.'

Modern India and Pakistan are also lands of contrast. In the villages families, though wrestling with poverty and ignorance, still preserve a traditional sense of loyalty in their relationships. Growing industrial conglomerations have resulted in people being cut off from these roots. Wider family circles become impoverished as the small family becomes the norm. More young mothers are lured to work long hours to raise their material standard of living. The Mothers' Union, a small force in a vast population, is tempted to be concerned only with the members' own spiritual welfare but it is trying to face up to the demands of society around it.

In many places church schools have closed down and Christian parents are left with an even greater responsibility for their children's upbringing. The Mothers' Union has for some years run a Brides' School in India where a succession of girls come to learn home-making skills and the spiritual basis of happy family life.

Over the years Mothers' Union members and their families have been caught up in wars and civil disorders throughout the world. Even while emergency regulations were in force in Kenya, a diocesan president with an intimate knowledge of their language was hard at work starting branches among the disaffected Kikuyu.

South African members include many of different colour and backgrounds. Workers do all they can to draw them into genuine unity. They feel inadequate for the magnitude of the task. One reports that she can only manage to visit the branches in her area once a year. Mothers' Union gatherings draw together, as far as conditions permit, all races. For many it has been the only chance to get to know personally women on the other side of the great divide.

As it happened a Central President was once able to share in person the sufferings of some families in South Africa. Mrs Basil Roberts was visiting Johannesburg in 1960 when shootings took place in the African township a few miles out. Several members were among those wounded. At the multi-racial Festival Service in the cathedral next day, the absence was deeply felt of those who were 'too busy crying for their dear ones'. Mrs Roberts went on to Pretoria. The police swooped at dawn on many homes, arresting people of all ages. Mothers' Union members were again involved.

The civil war in Nigeria caused great concern to the society. Members were forced to leave their homes and became refugees. There was no word for some weeks of the whereabouts of the Mothers' Union worker. When she could get news out, she was found using her car for relief work. Members, she reported, who themselves had survived, had lost most or all their possessions but were doing all they could to help the old and young children.

The present Central President, Mrs Susan Varah, began her term of office by attending the West African Mothers' Union Provincial Council in Ibadan. She shared in plans being made for a home to look after a few of the many children orphaned by the civil war. She put the idea to members in the United Kingdom and other countries who could offer help. Younger members worked particularly hard to raise money for the venture. The home was started in a reconditioned war-torn house belonging to the hospital, with Pearl and Ken Campbell as 'mother' and 'father'. Some two years later a new home had been built with the gifts of members in many countries. Mrs Treadgold, the chairman of the Young Members' Committee at the Mary Sumner House, went to Nigeria to be present at the opening. 'The children were delighted with the gift of felt pens I took with their names on them,' she reported.

The Nigerian authorities wished all orphans to be fostered or adopted by families. But we are still to be responsible for the welfare and education of these children and if finally university or technical training is necessary, this will also be our responsibility. The Campbells set about finding homes for the children among local people who had taken an interest in the home. For one of the little boys there was a happy ending. 'By a week before Christmas arrangements had been made for everyone except Ebere, then we had a message to say that his "father" was coming to see us! Early the following day he arrived, there was no doubt that he actually was Ebere's father—it was so touching to witness their reunion. During the war Ebere had been put in a Feeding Centre since the family could find no food and three of their children had already died; after the war their father had tried in vain to trace him and in the end had presumed he was dead. What a joy it was to take Ebere to Enugu where his family are now living and reunite him with his mother, sister and brothers?'

8

WORLD-WIDE FELLOWSHIP

'L'union fait la force'

UNION is strength, or sometimes, l'union fait la force was one of Mary Sumner's maxims. As she looked round at the end of her life on the world-wide family she had brought into being, her vision had come true in undreamed-of ways. Women of many countries had grown close together, not only in spiritual bonds but through their concern for the whole of life, body, mind and spirit.

The ladies of the 1880s set about teaching homecraft and the care of children to the 'cottage mothers' who were being drawn to the society. Right up to the present day, workers in many parts of the world find themselves plunged into practical teaching in the cause of Christian family life. What is the point, for instance, of producing uplifting literature for women who cannot read? As recently as 1967, teaching weeks for Indian village women included a daily session of instruction in reading and writing. In some branches probationers affirm their promises by making thumb marks. The problems of electing a committee are simplified when all those who are able to read are put on it.

Food looms large in the welfare of families where wages are low or non-existent, where floods and drought can destroy the harvest. Mothers' Union workers find themselves sharing a strange variety of meals when they visit the homes of members. As well as teaching the best use of the few resources available for feeding families, they find themselves learning a great deal about sacrifice and generosity.

A Brides' School in Bangladesh asked the girls attending

76

to bring enough rice for their three days' stay. It sounds little to those used to attending conferences in more affluent countries. 'The months of May to August are probably the leanest months for the people of our district, only the rich have rice in their store houses and the poor have to buy it from meal to meal. To feed reasonably well they have two rice meals a day, but at this time of the year most of them can only afford one. So to give your daughter a good supply of rice for three days is indeed a sacrifice; and, of course, this same daughter could probably have earned her own rice by working at the rich farmer's house during the days she would spend at the school.'

Sometimes, it must be admitted, visitors to Mothers' Union occasions, even in areas where food is normally hard to come by, are overwhelmed by the generous hospitality they are shown. In Bechuanaland 'part of an ox had been sent down by Chief Oteng Mphoeng, while mealie meal and sugar arrived from the churchwarden's store, and our mothers had collected cash for tea, milk, jam and beans.'

Branch programmes in countries overseas often pay more attention to culinary matters than at home. It is the Mothers' Union that holds an annual cookery competition on a West Indian island. Women with well-appointed town kitchens compete with members who live in ramshackle conditions in the villages. It is a relief to learn that these occasions are marked by 'a real Mothers' Union spirit of fellowship'.

A worker in South Africa finds malnutrition an ever-increasing problem. 'Often the diet is mainly of porridge made from mealie meal and water, and includes no milk, little meat and few vegetables. The result is that people are often mentally dull and unresponsive, physically tired and lacking in effort. Much teaching in Mothers' Union meetings is therefore given to food and its preparation.'

Occasionally a more developed country finds itself needing to give practical instruction. A worker in Australia was assigned to the problems of black-skinned aborigines whose traditional way of life was threatened by the extenison of cattle stations into their territories. 'They have never slept under a roof, nor worn a stitch of clothing.' Through vigorous action taken by the Church, it was agreed that they should be integrated into Australian society. 'This means feeding, clothing, educating and training them in skills, and helping them by every means to accomplish in a generation or two what normally takes centuries.'

All members everywhere give a large part of their meeting time to grasping the implications of the Christian faith for themselves and their families. It seems as if the world would not hold the books that could be written as to how each branch works this out in its own life. An account from the worker in Guayana must suffice to demonstrate features found in most branch programmes in one way or another.

'In Mothers' Union we try to be truly what Mary Sumner planned—"The handmaid of the Church". "Those wicked ants" said a priest, "they have been at work damaging the building again, we must find some more money to stop the little creatures from doing their big work", and he fixes a steady gaze on the Enrolling Member of his Branch. A few weeks later he is asked to be Chairman at a Concert and arrives to find a packed hall, all the tickets having been sold by the members, who have also worked hard providing the items and the refreshments. At the end of it all, the amount was handed in to stop the ants' feast-day!

' "How can you Mothers' Union members always do so well?" asked the Warden of the youthful Enrolling Member. "When we try fund-raising it is always a fund-sinking!" "Well!" she replied, "we always begin with prayer and then we go on to plan and to work." That really is our keynote. We try to make our prayer life strong and trusting.

'Our meetings are usually well attended; we are at times a study circle, we read and study our Bible and our

Faith, and also the literature of our Organisation. This we do with a great variety of methods, so that there is nearly always a surprise waiting for those who come to the meeting, tired, after rushing around to get all done in the home before setting out. Our members find there is much laughter and fun and not a dull moment while they learn again what they had forgotten, or something new about the Bible or the Church. We are sometimes a working party—making vestments and Altar linen or covering kneelers. At other meetings we learn handicrafts of different kinds—the making of fruit bowls out of old gramophone records, reading lamps out of cowhorns, etc.

'Hospital visiting is also done by the members, especially among the Amerindian patients who are so lonely and far removed from their relatives and friends. A rota is formed—each Branch during one day in the week—so that no day of the week is without visiting being done by members of the Mothers' Union.

'We have now started a "Cradle Roll", by which each Branch undertakes to visit every baby baptised in the Church during the month, and invite the mother, if possible, to join the Mothers' Union.'

Some of the newer methods employed would have surprised earlier generations. In one East African country there is a regular half-hour television programme run by the local Mothers' Union. Once an English member wrote a play based on a story told her by an African which members acted themselves, hoping to promote discussion of family problems among viewers.

Throughout the development of the work overseas home members have poured out financial help and workers in a steady stream. Transport is provided. Money is made available for conferences, training schemes and special ventures. There has been a warm response from the recipients of such help with expressions of genuine gratitude and affection. As the decades have passed, the tone changes. There is less talk of dutiful daughters and loving white mothers and more of women united in concern for family life in their different settings. As responsibility is handed over increasingly to local leadership, good relationships have been maintained. When a European worker retires to be replaced by a national, there are genuine expressions of affection and thanksgiving.

The relationship between the parts of the whole has been firmly based in prayer and friendship that is not merely generalised good will but has personal links between women who have often become close friends across great distances.

The regular observance of the Wave of Prayer has resulted in the toing and froing of letters and personal visits between, say, Oxford in England and Owerri in Nigeria or between Accra and Dublin. Presents are constantly exchanged. Members in the British Isles design and make a banner for 'their' cathedral overseas. Carved or woven objects are brought over to Britain. Men travelling the world on business find themselves carrying strange parcels at the behest of their womenfolk.

The Overseas Department at the Mary Sumner House has in addition a scheme linking individual branches with each other. Most branches in the British Isles are in regular touch with one overseas. The traffic between two branches can become entirely personal. One member can know the names of members far away and can share something of their family joys and tribulations. At least one branch in Britain has set itself to learn the language of its linked branch so that the simple courtesy of speaking in the other's tongue is not all one-sided.

Proceeds from Overseas Sales in London and the dioceses in the United Kingdom reach high figures over and above the direct giving to overseas work which is expected of each member. In 1972 the Overseas Sale raised almost £13,000, for example, with an extra £500 from the Young Members'

Stall earmarked for the children's home in Nigeria. Overseas members play their part in efforts of this sort. On Tristan da Cunha, where every married woman is a Mothers' Union member, wool from the island flock is carded and spun and the knitted garments are sent on the August mail-boat. They will appear on the Overseas Stall at the sale in London in October.

The very generosity of the dioceses in Britain can sometimes obscure the important fact that basically all members are on terms of financial equality. On becoming a member every woman is expected to pay the tribute, as it is called, to finance the work of the society. In addition to this many dioceses that have previously been content to receive help from wealthier countries are making great efforts to raise more from their own members. One diocese where there is great poverty among many families has made a start by aiming to raise £100 for every £1,000 it receives from the Overseas Fund and is hoping gradually to increase this proportion.

More difficult to assess than financial support is the spiritual gain that comes from close links between women of different countries. In any conversation with members in Britain on the subject there is admiration for the quality of commitment in overseas branches. 'The Mothers' Union means so much to them. They even have a special uniform they wear to show they are members. And here we are, leaving our MU brooches in the drawer, even if we've got them.' 'The members of our linked branch walk miles and miles just to make their communion and meet together. It's just two minutes down the road for me and most of the time I don't bother.' 'In our linked diocese in Africa, there's a branch in every parish. One parish has fourteen, meeting in different villages. I wish we had that sort of enthusiasm here.'

It is challenging for any member anywhere to hear of a diocesan president in Africa who takes prospective leaders into her home for a fortnight at a time on a sort of informal training course. Melanesian members don't just worry about families on the verge of breaking up. They take them in to share their own home life until things can be sorted out, sometimes for as long as a year at a time.

There are special lessons for those linked to a branch in a leper colony. Members, they discover, are particularly glad of the chance to give thanks to God for the many blessings of their corporate life.

It is almost comforting to find that not all members in other lands are entirely perfect. Faults and shortcomings serve to bind the world-wide family together as effectively as virtues. Many an official in many places must have sympathised when she read in a copy of her *Mothers' Union News* a report of a teaching week: 'With twenty-one women the first week it seemed to be possible to get to know only the difficult ones. There were a number of these, but looking back one can only be conscious of and thankful to the Holy Spirit that with women from such different villages and of such an age range the squabbling was not greater.'

Central Presidents from Mary Sumner onwards have been the visible centre of the unity of all members. Successive holders of the office have increasingly interpreted this responsibility by undertaking frequent tours of the scattered parts of the world-wide fellowship. As the aeroplane has made it possible to cover distances more quickly, the demands of these journeys have become heavier on those undertaking them. In the course of a brief visit to South Africa, Mrs Roberts travelled over 8,000 miles and slept in fifty different beds. When Mrs Hallifax spent three busy weeks in India and Ceylon, some of her engagements were undertaken in temperatures of 94° Fahrenheit with 70 per cent humidity. This is how she spent two such days:

'My last two days were spent with Ann Biswas and the Bishop of Barrackpore who drove us north to Krishnagar and on through the beautiful country to Baliura, where the whole village again turned out to greet us. Then for the night to Doyahari hospital where I had my earliest ever Mothers' Union meeting—8 a.m.—and reluctantly left Sister Purchas and the hospital she runs so splendidly and so devotedly, to drive south through Calcutta to Mograhat, a small village off the road where the Bishop's car was impaled on a small hump bridge, and where we met Marjorie Stone and many members who had come in from the surrounding area.'

Whether they were taking part in discussions with provincial councils, sharing with huge crowds at festival services or meeting branch members in their own setting, Central Presidents found themselves again and again over-whelmed with the warmth of the affection and loyalty for the society they represented.

In 1955 Mrs Rosamund Fisher (now Lady Fisher) had come to the end of her term as Central President but when she visited Central Africa with her husband, then Arch-bishop of Canterbury, she was received by members of the Mothers' Union as a deeply respected leader. She wrote a letter to members in England, telling of her experiences. Here is the expression of fellowship, the mutual love that is freely given and accepted among members. It surmounts barriers of high office and of different backgrounds. Here is the authentic note of joy in meeting together, springing from the sharing of obedience in common discipleship of the Lord Jesus Christ.

'We arrived in Nyasaland and boarded the Ilala (600 tons) to go to Likoma. We had a good twelve hours' crossing to the island, arriving at 6 a.m. The whole popula-tion was on the shore or lining the path up to the Cathedral. Somehow it was very New Testament—the lake, the boat, the thousand or so on the shore! Down they knelt for the Archbishop's blessing, then rising, sang and clapped and stretched out brown hands to shake ours. We walked slowly up to the wonderful Cathedral, built like an Italian one on the hillside, of rather pink stone, with a tower and a cloister, and a smaller tower at its end; bougainvilleas and poinsettias making a riot of colour; the Cathedral bells (tubular) ringing out for the service. The Cathedral is 360 feet long and 50 feet wide—it was *packed*—not a place left for even one more piccaninny! Their little faces peered out over the low wall of the apse, large eyes gleaming in the dim light. 950 made their communion, priests administering at two side altars as well as at the high altar. The Archbishop celebrated in English, but all the singing was in their own language—such lovely singing. There seemed no difficulty in passing from one language to the other. All those who received the Sacrament had had to be at the Preparation Service, and none could communicate who had not got a ticket.

'We had breakfast, then while the Archbishop received gifts of eleven chickens and a ram (all alive!) and elephant tusks, I spoke to the Mothers' Union. They were glorious and so happy. After I had taken their photos they escorted me towards the main assembly under the trees, singing, clapping, dancing and 'Ullulahing''—I suddenly decided to ullulahe back! This caused a frenzy of delight and excitement—so much so that the policeman had to come hurrying to hush us!

'At Mpondas, all the way up to the place of meeting under a tree, the path was lined with children singing a little chant and, at intervals, bowing their heads. I gathered it was something like "Father, you have come, we greet you." They were too sweet, especially the tiny ones. A percussion band(?) of a drum and various tin instruments accompanied the singing. Here, after an address of welcome, we went into Church and they sang the Te Deum. I was in a side chapel with lots of mothers and some adorable small girls. The Archbishop blessed them there. During lunch the Mothers' Union launch was sighted and there was much excitement. I went down to get a cine picture of the landing. Then they had to feed, poor dears, and afterwards we had our meeting. The dear Bishop insisted upon coming to interpret for me.

'Here, they brought me four bead necklaces, a bracelet, several beaded milk jug covers, lots of eggs, and 2s. 8d. to buy myself some tea! I decided to put on my jewellery! And so I did, to shrieks of delight from the mothers. I ended by putting the milk covers on my hat! However, I had to take them off before I faced the *men* who would have thought it very frivolous! Everywhere I went the women pointed to the necklace and bracelet with delight and ullulahed as we left, so I gave them a counter demonstration which was well received!'

9

PUBLIC AFFAIRS

'Out of family life the nation grows'

IN July 1951 Mrs Remson Ward went to Brussels. This, one of the last engagements in her twenty years as Central Secretary, was to represent the Mothers' Union at the International Union of Family Organisations. The delegates, mostly men, including government officials, lawyers, doctors and representatives of family organisations in many countries, welcomed the delegate from the Mothers' Union as being 'especially representative of normal family life'. This was recognition of the work the society had undertaken for the well-being of all families from the earliest years of its existence.

Some time before women had begun to demand an equal place in society, Mothers' Union leaders were approaching men in public life on matters concerning the family and appearing on public platforms in support of causes they held dear. By 1912 a special committee had been appointed to be responsible for action on social problems. It has met regularly ever since and has studied many matters of public concern. Mary Sumner and her first colleagues evolved a method of tackling public issues as they appeared which has been extended and refined as the Mothers' Union expanded but which has remained the same in essence.

It depends on the maintenance of a two-way flow of information between branches and the Mary Sumner House. The centre provides definitive information and advice on matters that arise concerning families. Lectures by experts are arranged, conferences for an exchange of views, articles and pamphlets issued. When information is needed, the Mothers' Union can gather up findings from the wide spread of its branches. It alerts members to watch for problems that might arise in their own district and gives help in tackling them.

Sometimes a matter that has come to light in a particular area can be dealt with more effectively when taken up by the centre. A national service man was subjected to bullying, to the distress of his parents. The local branch reported the problem to the Mary Sumner House. The whole question of the conditions of young men during national service was discussed with the relevant authorities. This resulted in the Central President, Mrs Roberts, being invited to visit army and air force establishments to study conditions.

Official bodies are often prepared to give the society a sympathetic hearing as it has proved useful where information on family matters is needed. What do mothers think of the facilities provided by Child Welfare Clinics? What is the effect on young children of being taken from their parents and put into hospital? What goes on in teenage clubs? What effect does gambling have on family life? Civil servants, social workers and researchers who have needed factual answers to questions like that have enlisted Mothers' Union members in various places to find out.

Reports, white papers, private members' bills, all the flood of paper from government and administrative sources contain much that is relevant to the well-being of family life. The Mothers' Union can never afford to neglect the work of sifting through documents, analysing consequences and assessing trends: Its aim is always to form a corporate opinion as to what would benefit stable home life. Resolutions are passed and sent to appropriate authorities. Delegations appear before commissions and committees. Evidence is submitted and protests launched.

Members undertaking this aspect of the work became well-informed on public affairs. Mothers' Union publications

carry regular information to keep them in the picture. At
least one social worker takes the *Mothers' Union News*
regularly for its extracts from Hansard of debates concerning
the family and for its useful summaries of reports like
Seebohm on the social services or Newsom on education.

It did not take the Mothers' Union long to realise that its
hand would be strengthened if it worked with other bodies
who shared its views on particular issues. It has been joined
in protest and action with a long list of other societies, the
Magistrates' Association, the National Council of Women,
the Public Morality Council and many others.

In recent years the Mothers' Union meets regularly with
the Inter-Faith Group it established with representative
Roman Catholic, Free Church and Jewish women. Matters
of common concern come before it for study and any joint
action that seems advisable. It has undertaken social inquiries such as a recent pilot survey on communication
between parents and children.

A major concern felt by Mary Sumner herself became one
of the first issues to be taken up by the Mothers' Union. The
card she had printed for the early Old Alresford meetings
included, 'You are strongly advised never to give your
children beer, wine or spirits without the doctor's orders, or
to send young people to the public-house.'

In 1900 she was writing to all diocesan presidents asking
them to bring the matter of children in public houses to the
attention of all their members. There was about this time a
demand from political bodies for legislation to prevent
children from entering public houses altogether. When the
Mothers' Union's support was sought, the Central Council
reluctantly decided that to come out in public behind this
particular campaign would give the impression that the
society was entering into party politics. It has always sought
to ensure that women of different political persuasions could
share in its work and witness. The Mothers' Union members
were urged to take seriously the 'cruel wrong which is being

done to the children by allowing them to enter the Public Houses'. Even when legislation was passed to regulate the conduct of public houses, the society remained vigilant about the effect of alcohol on young people. This problem has not been solved. Recent statistics show that cases of alcoholism among young people is increasing at an alarming rate. No doubt present-day members are even now brooding over the matter.

They have recently taken action on a related issue, the misuse of drugs among young people. Conferences have been held in various centres when parents met with social workers and those working in the field of addiction. Teachers and medical authorities were invited to talk over mutual problems in the matter. The Mothers' Union produced pamphlets, giving facts about drugs, which were widely distributed. One result of the discussions was a list of treatment centres which was made readily available to those dealing with young people.

In Mary Sumner's day registry offices in the big centres of population could be used as 'agencies for evil'. Unsuspecting girls looking for work might find themselves being used as prostitutes. The Mothers' Union lent its voice to the move to establish a chain of reputable registry offices to which decent girls could go without danger. At the same time it put pressure on local authorities and police to make regular inspections of dubious establishments and take necessary measures to put them out of business. The efforts, along with others in the field, produced the 1906 Act which brought employment registries under official control.

Reading matter suitable for the family circle has always been a preoccupation of the society. A vigilant eye has been kept on literature considered unsuitable for young people. Specific examples that were considered to contravene laws of decency have been referred to police authorities. While they have not always seen eye to eye with the society as to what constitutes pornographic literature, they have welcomed the opportunity to discuss problems with representative parents.

In 1949 the Mothers' Union was troubled at a spate of childrens' comics which seemed not only lacking in good taste but positively offensive in their encouragement of violence. A conference was held at the Mary Sumner House which included teachers, probation officers and parents. The Minister of Education was approached. Though sympathetic, he took the view that any undermining of the traditional freedom of the press might result in greater harm.

Moral teaching has always been in the forefront of Mothers' Union minds when considering their responsibilities for their children. In their view sex instruction should not be undertaken in isolation but in the context of the whole background of loving family relationships. The parents' responsibility in the matter is paramount. Mary Sumner often spoke of the need for teaching on these matters, a brave thing to do for a lady of gentle upbringing at a time when such things were never mentioned in public. Nowadays the wheel has come full circle. The society is faced with the opposite problem. In days of constant public display of sexual matters, its plea is usually for restraint and reticence.

A piece of legislation which the Mothers' Union supported to a successful conclusion was the Act passed in 1912 to stamp out white slave traffic. The society had suggested amendments to the proposed Bill to make it more effective. Resolutions from diocesan presidents had been sent to their Members of Parliament, urging them to support the proposed legislation.

In these days when many responsible people are perturbed at the increase in the world population it is strange to look back on 1913 when the Archbishop of York was addressing the Mothers' Union on the grave consequences of a declining birth-rate. A sub-committee was set up to consider the matter but the following years brought too many worries about the appalling death-rate for it to take much action.

It did report to the Central Council in 1919 and a resolution was passed:

'The Central Council of the Mothers' Union holds that, as for all normal married persons, it is a duty, and an honour, to accept God's gift of a family; a selfish limitation of children is wrong, and that all artificial checks to conception are against the laws of Nature.'

At the time of the 1926 Constitution, Fundamental Principles on Marriage and the Family were set down on paper. This resolution was adopted as one of the paragraphs, with 'refusal' being substituted for 'limitation'. By 1946, with the increased use of contraceptives, the position of the society was being increasingly questioned. A sentence was added, carefully designed to hold the fort while leaving doors open. 'While upholding this ideal, the Mothers' Union has never made view on birth control a test of membership.'

All members were concerned when contraceptives went on public display. In some places they could be obtained from slot machines. The Mothers' Union was anxious about the effect on young people. It took strong action to support a bill in Parliament which sought to control the display and advertisement of contraceptives but this was talked out at the second reading. Members were alerted to study the problem in their own areas and to urge their local authorities to enforce bye-laws which controlled the marketing of contraceptive devices. Subsequent moves to prescribe the pill to girls at an early age without discussion with their parents have been queried with the Minister responsible.

In the 1920s the society was concerned with the legal age for marriage, which it considered too low at fourteen for boys and twelve for girls. Representatives appeared before a select committee of the House of Lords. The 1929 Act which raised the minimum age to sixteen for both boys and girls was welcomed by the Mother's Union.

As more mothers took up full-time employment, the effect on their young children was the subject of close study.

Members in various areas set about finding out what
arrangements were made for the care of children and
whether they were adequate. They helped to uncover the
dangers of children wandering the streets after school or
letting themselves in to empty houses.

The Mothers' Union, with women of other Churches,
made strong representations in favour of Family Allowances.
It co-operated with the Health Service in producing information about the welfare of children in hospital and the
working of the maternity services.

The shortage of nurses had its effect on labour wards in
some hospitals. Women were left alone, often for hours at a
time. In 1962 the Mothers' Union began quietly exploring
the possibilities of training suitable members to sit with
women in labour while the nursing staff was busy elsewhere.
Some hospitals took up the idea enthusiastically and a rota
of members has been drawn up who undertake this work
regularly.

It was hardly possible for the Mothers' Union to avoid
being drawn into the debate about abortion. While it has
never taken a public stand against abortion, it deplores the
view that it should be a service on demand to all wishing to
avail themselves of it.

The International Travellers' Aid offers help to girls who are
coming in increasing numbers to take jobs with British
families. For the last twenty years Mothers' Union members
have shared in the rota of helpers manning kiosks provided by
British Rail at London main-line stations. Here are some of
the human problems that came the way of a helper at
Victoria:

'A young girl coming to live "Au Pair" with a family
to learn English finds no one to meet her.

'An elderly Yugoslav woman gets out of the train
thinking she is in Bradford where her son lives; she has
no idea what to do next, and speaks only Serbo-Croat.

'Seven West Indian children arrived at Victoria from

Genoa. Their families in Manchester and Leeds were not expecting them until the next day and had not come to London to meet them.

'A Hungarian woman travelling home was found in great distress because her Travel Visa through Europe had expired; she had no money and her daughter lived in Nottingham.'

No one can concern themselves with family life without having their hearts wrung by the inadequate conditions in which many families are forced to live. The problem has been with the Mothers' Union throughout its life. As direct action in providing more and better accommodation must be undertaken at a local level, diocesan officials have been encouraged to take an active part in housing associations in their areas, working with groups from all the Churches. Some concentrate on housing for the elderly, some on young families, and some on such special needs as those of unsupported mothers.

When, in the years after the 1945 war, there was a public outcry at the conditions endured by homeless families in the Greater London area, some branches suggested that mothers and children might welcome a day out from the reception centres when members in the country round London would entertain them. The idea caught on. The Church Army provided transport. The visiting families usually lunched in members' homes and gathered for tea-parties in summer gardens with games for the children and a lot of talk among the mothers. One account would indicate that the receiving was not all on one side:

'The value of the day was not only in giving a happy time to our guests in their day out from their drab surroundings but it did make us all, as members of the Mothers' Union, realise how much we have to be thankful for. We know that this one day was only a very small effort on our part to try to show less fortunate people that we all belong to God's family. But it left us with an aching void—what can we do *more* to see that people have adequate housing to bring up their families in a Christian way? Must more of us who can launch out from our "cosy monthly meetings" into local government or other social services where we can use our Christian influence?'

While the Mothers' Union as a whole has studied particular issues and initiated joint action, its branches at local level have found their own different ways to be of service in their local communities. This work was given extra impetus by the observance in 1963 of a Christian Family Year. As Mrs Hallifax, Central President at the time, told a press conference, 'Christian Family Year was a positive and sincere attempt to focus intelligent interest on the Christian concept of family life.'

A great variety of acts of service were started or extended from this period. Creches and play-groups were set up. Some are designed to enable mothers to do their shopping while their children are cared for. Nursery tents are organised at big events from Royal Shows to a miners' gala. At one hospital children are minded while their mothers donate blood. While mothers visit their husbands in one prison, their children are kept occupied. A multi-racial play-group is designed to bring children of different races together.

The Mothers' Union gives help to immigrant families where it can, teaching English to women in their homes and making friends with newcomers in their midst. The Overseas Fund pays the salaries of two workers among immigrant communities in English cities.

Members are regular visitors in hospitals of all kinds, old peoples' homes, children's homes and private houses where there are few callers. Branches entertain mothers with handicapped children, disabled children, new arrivals in the community, students who are far from home, anyone they find in need of a friendly welcome.

The work of fostering children, specially those not easy to place, is undertaken by some members. It was this need that Mr R. A. Butler, Home Secretary at the time of Christian Family Year, brought to the notice of his audience at the Parents' Meeting in the Albert Hall. 'There are over 60,000 children in the care of local authorities in England and Wales. Some of them will be in care for only a short time, perhaps while mother is in hospital, but many will spend most of their childhood in care and for them it is important to provide something as near a real home as possible.'

In 1947 one member and her husband put a bed up in their son's bedroom and took a boy through the local Children's Officer to be a brother to their own. By 1966 they had two grown-up foster sons and a boy of fifteen living with them, and several others regularly bringing 'grandchildren' to see them. They had obviously found great happiness on the way.

In the 1970s a scheme called Away from It All was well under way. Mothers in need of a rest and a break could be put in touch with members in the country or by the sea who are willing to offer hospitality. One branch came to the conclusion that families would benefit more from a time to be together with the usual pressures removed. They raised money to equip a caravan for the use of families referred to them as being in need of a holiday.

Some districts have been circulated with offers of help at times of family crisis. The members willing to answer any calls have found themselves with a variety of jobs. They look after families when the mother has a new baby. They arrange transport to hospitals and schools. They do family shopping and keep the house clean where the mother is ill. This kind of service is proving particularly valuable in new housing areas, where young mothers are often far from relatives who could help families in emergencies of this sort.

When the cinema made its first tentative appearance, the Mothers' Union was not impressed. Attitudes changed as it gained a hold on the spare time of the nation. Among the women flooding in to Mothers' Union branches, there were no doubt many who enjoyed a night out at the pictures. By 1916 Central Council was looking into regulations governing cinematograph shows. By 1926 a sub-committee was in existence which watched the trends in new films as they appeared. Today any press showing of new films will include in the audience one or two Mothers' Union film visitors. They will review new films for *Home and Family* and *Mothers' Union News*, making special mention of any they consider suitable for family entertainment.

The society has made a special study of the effect of the cinema on young children. Children's Film Clubs are frequently visited. In 1950 the society was invited to submit evidence to the Departmental Committee studying Children and the Cinema. It welcomed the setting-up of the Children's Film Foundation and has maintained close relationships with it since.

Successive secretaries of the British Board of Film Censors have proved grateful for the Mothers' Union's interest in films and have several times been present at discussions in the Mary Sumner House. In 1972 the Mothers' Union took to the Board the concern felt throughout the society about the increase of brutal violence depicted in such films as *The Devils*, *Clockwork Orange* and *Straw Dogs*. The Central President backed these discussions with a letter to the Home Secretary and to those responsible for making and showing films of this sort. They hoped that a solution might be found in making a greater variety of films available so that families could choose those they felt would be most profitable and entertaining.

When television came, it too was not immediately welcomed with open arms but the Mothers' Union came to the view that it could be used for positive ends, widening horizons and giving entertainment in the home. The various reports and proposed changes in television over the last few years have been studied closely by those responsible for this work at the centre and in the dioceses.

Television-watching groups are trained to take an intelligent interest in programmes. They learn how television works, how its budget affects the material it puts out, who is responsible for programmes, how best to convey criticism and appreciation. They submit reports annually to the Mary Sumner House of series and individual programmes they have watched.

Their views are by no means those of the moralists who protest loud and often against programmes they dislike personally, Here is the chairman of the Central Television, Radio and Cinema Group reporting on a controversial television BBC series, *The Family*:

'The BBC have, after all, a duty under their Charter to "inform and educate" as well as "to entertain", and if *The Family* was not entertainment it was certainly informative. We in the Mothers' Union have a special concern for the family, and those of us who watched this documentary may not have enjoyed it, but it surely must have made us think very hard about the sort of life that a large section of our population have to endure, mostly through economic circumstances and no fault of their own.'

Both BBC and Independent Television have formed a high opinion of the value of the Mothers' Union's work. They encourage their staff to give technical help and advice and have proved themselves ready to listen to what the society has to tell them.

When Lord Hill was chairman of the Independent Television Authority, he entertained at its headquarters some two hundred of the Mother's Union's television watchers who were encouraged to question closely and sometimes critically a team of his top men. At one point Lord Hill told his assembled guests: 'It has been said that television is the most marvellous way of doing nothing, yet it is a window on the world presenting to many a new outlook, new angles, new entertainment and has been an immense contribution to human happiness—but much needs to be done. Criticise, seek to improve it, but don't take refuge in global statements.'

That last sentence might be the motto of the work of the Mothers' Union in public affairs. Criticise—it has often been forced into criticism when so much seemed to threaten family life. Seek to improve—it has tried all through its hundred years. Don't take refuge in global statements. True, there had been a good deal of talk over the years about sanctity and fellowship and purity but the Mothers' Union has been conscientious in translating what it believes into hard informed work on behalf of the larger community.

10

MISSION TO YOUNG MOTHERS

'There is special need . . .'

'THERE is special need for enlisting the interest and help of
the young mothers of today, for they have to meet the many
new problems, both in religious and in social questions, and
their advice and co-operation is of the greatest use in dealing
with these difficulties.'

Mary Sumner was over ninety when she wrote this appeal
for younger women to support the Mothers' Union. She was
aware of the dilemma that the society faced. The fellowship
which was a mark of its corporate life became ever more
valuable to the members as they grew to old age. Yet the
very devotion of its older members could result in the society
being unattractive to younger women.

She rejected any suggestion of an age limit for membership. 'I am afraid . . . that you have hardly realised the
double basis of our Mothers' Union—Prayer and Work.
The grandmothers and great-grandmothers whom you
mention have more time in their old age to pray for "children
and children's children", and we have always felt that these
prayers uphold and strengthen the younger mothers in their
anxious work of training their little ones, and that they
bring untold blessing on the whole Society.

'It would be a fatal weakness to oust these aged members,
and, speaking from personal knowledge of our members, I
know how enormously they value the great bond of union in
prayer.'

As early as 1912 there was a proposal for a separate Young
Wives' League to cater particularly for young women after

they were married and before they had children. During the war years a special committee set about fact-finding on the position of younger women in the Mothers' Union. In 1917 a Young Wives' Committee was set up, with responsibility for work among younger women.

Archbishop Randall Davidson and his wife entertained a conference of young wives and mothers at Lambeth Palace which set up a Young Wives' Fellowship to be closely linked with the Mothers' Union, aiming to attract younger educated women. The Central Council reacted cautiously, not convinced of the wisdom of limiting the new venture to one particular class. It won't go down well in the north, one delegate told them. But soon they forgot their doubts and all dioceses were being urged to set up Young Wives' Fellowships.

By 1919 the Fellowships had 600 members. As in future efforts among younger women, they laid more emphasis than the parent body on work among husbands and wives together. Before long they came under criticism for their apparent lack of success in bringing their members into the Mothers' Union. By the end of 1920 the Young Wives' Fellowships were convinced that they needed a separate existence. Not all the women they were attracting were members of the Church of England. Though most would accept Christian ideals of marriage in a general way, many were not happy with the Mothers' Union's interpretation of qualifications for membership.

Their discussions with the Mothers' Union were friendly. By a narrow majority the Central Council granted affiliation to Young Wives' Fellowships, though it grew increasingly uneasy and finally withdrew affiliation in 1937 when it considered that the Fellowships had become too ambivalent on the matter of divorce. This left a gap in Mothers' Union work. It was felt that the society appeared old-fashioned to young women of the post-war years. The Girls' Friendly Society which had close ties with the Mothers' Union underlined the need for action by pressing for some organisation under the Mothers' Union umbrella to which girls could be referred on their marriage.

Another committee brooded and in 1920 came up with the suggestion of a Fellowship of Marriage which would take in newly married women as well as mothers of young children. This time, they insisted, anyone joining the new movement must be made an integral part of the parent body by signing the same membership card as Mothers' Union members. By 1921 when the Fellowship of Marriage was officially launched, its first members had already made their mark, studying education in schools, training young speakers and visiting new mothers in hospital.

It was not long before they were wondering if fathers could become full members of the Fellowship of Marriage. The Mothers' Union was faced with a dilemma. It was obvious that men in full sympathy with its objects would prove of great strength to its witness but if men joined the Fellowship of Marriage they would *ipso facto* become members of the Mothers' Union. Clearly the society would change its identity. In the end the decision was made that the union of mothers should continue to be such but that wherever possible men should be drawn in to share its work and fellowship.

The Fellowship of Marriage was established in many parishes. It also proved useful in drawing together younger women in wider areas such as deaneries where it served as a training ground for Mothers' Union leaders and speakers. It saw fellowship as threefold, between husband and wife, between parents and children and fellowship among its members based on their common discipleship.

By 1935 the Fellowship was summoning its members to tackle the inevitable problem. The younger people who had joined originally were no longer so very young. Yet the strength of the bonds between them made it hard for their members to move into the Mothers' Union branches. The solution that emerged was simple to grasp and somewhat painful to operate. Membership of the Fellowship of Marriage was to be for women under forty. It was hoped that its leaders would be under forty-five. The Central Council of the Mothers' Union accepted this recommendation but urged its own branches to play their part. They must take steps to make their meetings attractive to women who would be displaced from the Fellowships. In particular branches should provide opportunities for discussion on subjects of contemporary concern in the community.

Not all Enrolling Members regarded the work of the Fellowship of Marriage with full sympathy. It appeared to them to be a means of creaming off the more energetic younger women who might otherwise become branch members. It was also rejected by some incumbents who were struggling to hack away the network of organisations that seemed to be threatening to strangle parochial life. Such clergymen preferred to 'stick to the Mothers' Union'.

Before another war resulted in a new direction being taken in work among young mothers, it is worth pausing to remark that the Fellowship of Marriage was to a great extent responsible for providing a generation of leaders to undertake the development of the post-war years.

An example of a Fellowship of Marriage in action comes from 1950 in Australia where it persisted after it had been superseded elsewhere. In a rapidly developing suburb, it specialised in drawing newcomers into the community. Shy ones were encouraged to contribute to discussions with their own kind on children and family life. Its library was particularly valued as books were not always easy to come by. To its leaders its great virtue was that it ensured a steady stream of youngish women into the Mothers' Union branch when they had grown past the Fellowship.

In 1941 the Central President, Mrs Theodore Woods, was urging the society to plan ahead. Mrs Helena Lambert, chairman of the Fellowship of Marriage, pleaded for a great effort to bring in to the Mothers' Union younger women who would be responsible for rebuilding society after the war. The Central Secretary, Mrs Remson Ward, spoke with passionate concern of the multitudes of young mothers outside the influence of the Church and ignorant of the Christian gospel. A campaign was launched with the twofold aim of drawing in to the Mothers' Union younger women who agreed with its principles and of getting in touch with those right outside the Church. Committees were set up in the dioceses and the support of the clergy was enlisted.

The Campaign Committee at the Mary Sumner House became concerned at the effect of war conditions on young mothers. They had a sympathetic hearing from the women Members of Parliament. The Ministry of Health promised all possible help bearing in mind the shortage of hospital beds and of nurses and midwives. The Minister of Labour was approached about the conditions of work of pregnant women.

Meanwhile in the dioceses the ventures of the new Campaign Committees were becoming entangled with existing Fellowships of Marriage. In 1945 the Fellowship of Marriage went into voluntary liquidation. The Mothers' Union moved into the post-war years with a new Young Members' Department which was responsible for work among younger women. It set about its two main tasks. Branches were helped to arrange their activities so that younger women would be attracted to membership. Open groups were started which would aim to draw together young mothers with no religious affiliations and to bring them closer to the Church.

Twenty years on the Young Members' Committee at the centre was presenting a memorandum to Central Council which indicates how this twofold purpose had been achieved. During 1966 6,000 young women were known to have been drawn into the life of the Church through the efforts of Young Wives' Groups. Just under 2,500 had been enrolled into the Mothers' Union from Young Wives' Groups.

The discrepancy between these two figures seems to have remained fairly constant throughout the years. A continuing problem has been that members of Young Wives' Groups are reluctant to leave their groups. The aim is that group members should have children of school age or under but difficulties arise where women with little knowledge of the Christian faith join the Group. Even if there is a Mothers' Union branch in the parish that is ready and willing to accept younger women, the transition to full membership is impossible to regulate by rule of thumb.

Often such fellowship is created in Young Wives' Groups that their members would resist any attempt to break it. One young mother tells of the companionship she found when she went to live in a village where she knew nobody. In particular she found understanding help with bringing up her children. 'One of my little boys had always been to me a problem child, and I was almost always worried about him, sometimes in complete despair. I found that after my very first Group meeting I returned home with a great confidence that I would be able to cope with the children. My confidence dwindled after a few days, and made me look forward to the next meeting more than ever. I found that confidence increasing after subsequent meetings, and now, besides being more patient and tolerant, I have really learnt to enjoy my children.'

Others found comfort in adversity. 'There is an old saying "A fellow-feeling makes us wondrous kind," and it is perhaps because so many of the members of our group have had deep personal sorrows that the feeling of fellowship and sympathy is so apparent amongst our members. We are twenty-eight in number and four of us have known the sorrow of losing a child. One little girl was killed most tragically by a van backing as she was playing on the grass verge near her home. Two other members have children who are not quite normal mentally, a grief it must indeed be hard to bear. Another member has a little boy who had to be away from home for four years, suffering from a T.B. hip . . . .'

Objections to joining the Mothers' Union are not usually on ideological grounds but spring more from reluctance to leave Young Wives' Groups. As Mrs Sybil Canadine, first chairman of the Young Members' Committee, explained to a 1950 meeting of Enrolling Members: 'The Mothers' Union in itself is acceptable and many young mothers in Groups join the Mothers' Union. At first they implement their membership by attending Group meetings and they are encouraged to attend Branch services, corporate communion services and Branch meetings. A good many do this and for a time go to Group meetings and to Branch meetings as well. This overlapping or interlocking principle is a very good one.'

The most successful transition is probably when a whole Group becomes part of a branch with the Young Wives' Group Leader becoming Assistant Enrolling Member. A fresh start is made with a younger leader attracting younger women to the Group.

The needs of younger mothers have brought pressure on Mothers' Union branches and many have adjusted their programmes as the result. Times of meetings have become more flexible; arrangements for children are made; discussion of subjects of contemporary concern have begun to appear more frequently in branch programmes.

Young Wives' Groups come in great variety, ranging from a hundred women in a church hall to a few people renting a room in the local pub on a housing estate. One in an affluent suburb musters over forty at its meetings which move from one house to another with a supply of cups and folding chairs stacked in a member's garage ready to be taken round. In one new housing area young mothers pushed their prams over still unmade roads to foregather in the house occupied by a Mothers' Union member.

Group programmes vary. In theory they develop with the growing understanding of the members, though the recurring discussion of the 'static group problem' suggests that the impetus can be lost and the members fall into a rut. The principle has been to start where the young mothers are. Newcomers to Church matters will still respond to discussion of their children's spiritual needs. 'Telling Bible stories to children', 'What happens when your baby is baptised' or 'How to answer children's difficult questions' will interest most mothers. The next stage of presenting an adult faith can follow, 'Why is suffering allowed?' or 'Is there any point in prayer?'

Experienced group leaders insist that talking must be underpinned by action. Corporate prayer is welcomed by all mothers when it includes petitions for families among the Group who are in special need and thanksgiving for particular blessings. This can lead on to corporate silence, meditation on the scriptures and regular if simple rules for joint observance which become almost imperceptibly acceptance of practising membership of the Church.

Husbands are often drawn in to activities of Young Wives' Groups. Parents' meetings are arranged on subjects that affect all families in the area. In one diocese a husband-and-wives' committee has been appointed to develop this work.

Three examples demonstrate how groups have been developed by those sensitive to local opportunities.

In a market town in the south of England, Mothers' Union members started a club for young mothers who brought their babies to the local clinic. At first it was just a display of helpful literature and a chat over a cup of tea. Six years later it numbered over a hundred members.

'Five group meetings are held in different members' houses and mothers in the club who become members of the M.U. meet monthly with the Branch.

'We have our own tennis club, and mothers who thought they would never play tennis again, have taken it up with great enthusiasm. The Dramatic Group has drawn in others whose special interest lies in acting, and some who were teachers before they were married, have started Sunday Schools for the tinies in their own district. Others who are really keen on deepening their own spiritual lives, have met together for Bible Study and Prayer in one another's homes.

'In all the Club's activities, small children are catered for in a really practical way.'

One northern diocese has made a feature of Pram Groups.

'Most Pram Groups meet weekly. At the beginning of the month mothers and their tiny tots meet together in church for a Pram service. The three- and four-year-olds are encouraged to take an active part, they even take the collection! . . .

'The other meetings take place in the Parish Hall where the mums have an hour away from their children. They have a varied programme, they do not always want to be "talked at". They like to be involved in discussion, in actively preparing for, say, the Church Bazaar.'

A recently-formed group may indicate a new slant by helping people in need of support to find leadership among themselves. Mothers' Union members in a rural area were encouraged by local social workers to draw together a group of socially inadequate mothers, many of them under supervision under the 1963 Children and Young Persons Act. A playgroup is provided for the children.

'We now have 21 mothers, 38 children, and numbers of small babies who are a great attraction. Most of our mothers have between three and seven children. Seven mothers were living on their own, either separated or with husbands serving long prison sentences; this group felt deeply their inadequacy to take a double role. Three were cohabiting, and five were going through periods of matrimonial disharmony. Only two had reasonably stable marriages, one who originated from Glasgow, likened her isolated dwelling to living in the Sahara Desert.. One mother who has just joined the group had her first outing in three months when she was taken to a local clinic to avail herself of bathing facilities. . . .

'Mothers soon appointed their own secretary. Discussions on every conceivable problem have been enlightening. It has been an eye-opener for them to discover there were others in the same predicament, and to find that we, the helpers and officials, are mothers and women with our own problems to face. They help each other enormously by talking over their troubles.

'The mothers organise weekly "jumbles"; they pay for tea or coffee and biscuits. One mother brings her sewing machine and gives simple instructions on how to make and mend. The interested listen, the others gossip and relax. Another mum brought a hair dryer and we have hairdressing sessions. Now they want to make rugs, have a butcher tell them about choosing cuts of meat. In fact from wanting nothing but a few minutes peace, they have come to want all sorts of interesting things.'

In 1970 a seminar was held at the Mary Sumner House on Loneliness among Young Mothers. If anything was needed to confirm the society in its belief that work among young women of today is necessary, it would be found here. A consultant psychiatrist said: 'Much of modern housing conditions tend to increase loneliness, as so many young couples live far from their old backgrounds, and among strangers who are all trying to make their way in the world. Many young mothers feel guilty and frustrated at their loneliness, and believe themselves to be unique. Sometimes the more they feel this, the more difficult it is for them to talk to others, even to their husbands; their feelings of inadequacy make it impossible for them to break out of their dilemma.'

He was speaking to those who would understand when he told the Mothers' Union that the most important thing was bringing friendship to the young, using the 'intelligence of the heart'.

THE LEAN YEARS

IT would be hard to find a more unpopular cause in the 1960s than upholding the sanctity of marriage. Many were questioning the necessity for marriage as the basis of society. The old virtues of faithfulness and chastity were out of favour. Sexual experience was paramount, an obsessive feature of western society. The pursuit of personal happiness was held to be every man and woman's right.

Awakening a sense of responsibility in parents seemed a hopeless task. At an ever earlier age children refused to accept the standards of a previous generation. They demanded freedom to enter an alien world of their own. When it came to prayer and personal holiness, things were no easier. Traditional spiritual disciplines were largely neglected. Church going was on the decline. There was considerable interest in esoteric mysticisms but little sympathy for anything that could be defined and organised.

In one sense this served to strengthen the fellowship among Mothers' Union members as they felt themselves a minority under attack. They were sustained by the belief that they were not such a minority as might appear from press reports. For every marriage that ended in breakdown there were many more that survived the pressures of the modern world. For every young drop-out from society there was a far greater number growing up in mutual confidence with their parents. The Mothers' Union considered that it spoke for the majority of ordinary homes where families wanted to live together in peace and love.

What seemed to hit below the belt was the growing criticism of the society in Church circles which centred on the question of those women who were barred from membership because they had either themselves been a party to a divorce or had married a divorced man. Statistically the number of 'hard cases' who had to be denied membership had not kept pace with the rising divorce rate. Here and there officials had to wrestle with difficult problems. A woman newly arrived in a village goes to church and will, it is assumed, join the Mothers' Union. She might have to admit that she has re-married after divorce, a fact which might not otherwise have come to light.

But the rate of new members joining the Mothers' Union had slowed down until, by and large, only those able and willing to ally themselves with the objects of the Mothers' Union were seeking entry. The criticism from clergy and lay people arose from more complicated causes than women who were eager to join being denied membership. The Anglican Communion itself was changing its mind on the subject of its marriage disciplines, more quickly in some parts than in others. The general atmosphere was moving, in this as in other matters of theology, from definite doctrine to be faithfully preserved to a mood of re-assessment and questioning.

Not that there were many people in the Church who did not hold the fundamental principles of Christian marriage, the rock on which the Mothers' Union still stood firmly. The life-long relationship of one man with one woman was still the ideal for all couples and the standard which Christians were expected to achieve. What was under discussion was the way in which the Church dealt pastorally with the partners of marriages that had come to grief.

There was already sufficient evidence of the quality of second marriages, often more determinedly stable and loving because of the previous experience of unhappiness, for churchmen to feel uneasy at denying them the Church's approval. Even though a second marriage might not be possible in church, such couples ought to be received into full membership of the household of the faithful. This could be done at parish level except for the Mothers' Union branch. That door stayed firmly shut against any woman who had not been faithful to her marriage vows, regardless of the difficulties she might have encountered.

As the state's attitude to marriage legislation changed, theologians set about studying its implications for the Church's thinking and practice. The report of a Church of England Commission, *Putting Asunder*, accepted the principle of marriage breakdown as a cause for divorce. Previously one party had to be proved guilty of an offence against the marriage. The acceptance of this report by the Church Assembly in 1967 paved the way for the passing of the Divorce Reform Act in 1969, when marriage breakdown became accepted in the courts as a cause for dissolution of marriage.

Although the report had been careful to point out that its findings in no way affected the behaviour of Christians for whom life-long marriage was still the accepted norm, the situation became confused in the minds of many Church people. The idea of one partner being guilty of desertion or adultery or cruelty may have led to unseemly manipulation by those determined to obtain a divorce but it preserved the straightforward concept of right and wrong with the overtone of condemnation by society at large. When this was removed, Church members felt unsure of their attitudes to marriage discipline.

But the Mothers' Union did not change. It was still working on its 1926 Constitution. The parish clergy reacted sharply. Some vented their impatience with their own position as responsible churchmen in an ambivalent situation by attacking the society in their midst, accusing it of unchristian exclusiveness. Others came out with strong public support of the Mothers' Union's position, seeing it as part of a campaign to preserve standards that seemed to be slipping all round. Some incumbents drew close to their branch members in bonds of genuine suffering as they sought to reconcile what they had inherited as unchanging truth with the pastoral demands of the modern situation.

There was a move at this time among sympathetic clergy to reinforce the view that was held by some Mothers' Union members that, as the cause of lifelong marriage was under attack, the society should close its ranks and become even more uncompromising in its attitudes. Every society, the argument ran, has the right to lay down who should become members. A tennis club is not expected to open its doors to people who don't want to know one end of a racquet from another. If women didn't want to uphold the sanctity of marriage with all its implications, they need not come into the Mothers' Union.

It was far too late in its history for such an attitude to be practicable. By this time almost every parish had a branch. Even though recruitment was not at its former high level, the society still numbered a considerable body of church women among its members. Every shade of opinion within the Anglican Communion was represented within the society. If it were to overhaul its membership to become representative of only one stream of thought in the Church, it would cease to be recognisable as the Mothers' Union.

Inevitably discussion grew within the society itself as to the position of women of second marriages. The immediate problem seemed to many to be the growing divergence between the general practice of the Church and the rules of the Mothers' Union. If an incumbent, after consultation with his bishop, had admitted to communion a woman who had re-married after divorce, was the society justified in continuing to refuse membership to her? The denial was felt to be particularly hard as such families were often in greater need of support and friendship than those which had sailed in calmer waters.

Any body of people specifically pledged to maintain fellowship among themselves is ill-equipped to deal with deep internal divisions. The Mothers' Union proved no exception. Its instinct was to preserve the façade of unity when in fact disagreement was becoming widespread among the members. At this period the Mothers' Union was sharing with the Church and secular society a crisis of authority. Younger women were not content to be told by central authorities what they should and should not do. Things had changed from the days when an 1889 issue of *Mothers' Union Journal* had carried a series of 'Letters to a Young Mother from an Old Mother' containing good advice which it confidently expected would be followed.

The general atmosphere of the time was against rigorous systems of right and wrong. Psychological insights into human behaviour had resulted in a deeper understanding of the causes of failure in human relationships. While giving even more urgency to the need for families to be helped to achieve a stable healthy setting in which young people could grow to full maturity, it had become almost impossible for one human being to say to another, You must not follow this course of action; it is wrong. The more usual reaction to those who fell short of the ideal had become, There but for the grace of God. . . .

It is not easy to trace the course of the debate within the Mothers' Union at this period, as little was allowed to appear in official publications. From a rare voice heard in 1967, it seems that the way the society organised its affairs, still much as it had from its beginnings, was also coming under attack. 'The question of structure is, I think, vital. As an organisation the M.U. is geared to permanence when situations are transitory; to a hierarchy when the flavour of the times is egalitarian and democratic; to a partisan spirit when almost all churches are looking across denominational barriers; to protocol and precedent where flexibility and pragmatism may be needed.'

Certainly inherited structures were proving inadequate
for those longing for open discussion of deep problems facing
them in their spheres of work. The 1958 World-Wide Conference had again proved a genuine experience of fellowship
for those coming from many countries but the business
sessions were a disappointment for some who had hoped that
the nettle of growing disaffection could be grasped. Too often
delegates found themselves discussing trivia in public and
worrying together about major issues in corridors.

It was on the international scale that difficulties about
bars to membership were seen at their most acute. The
different countries were developing their own rules in church
and state for dealing with marriages that had run into acute
difficulty. As the society at home was shrinking, membership
in many places overseas was still on the increase. The voice
of those from outside the United Kingdom became increasingly powerful.

The Anglican Church in Canada was the first to introduce
a canon permitting re-marriage in church after divorce in
certain carefully defined cases. Its status as an equal associate
with the other provinces of the Anglican Communion made
a development of this sort possible. The Mothers' Union
in Canada found itself in a difficult position.

The majority of its members was happy to accept that all
women married in church should be eligible to become
members of the Mothers' Union, but under the 1926
Constitution some would now be married in church who
would not be eligible for Mothers' Union membership.
The Canadian Mothers' Union as a whole decided to stand
in line with the practice of its Church and thus ceased to be
affiliated to the parent body. Mothers' Union work was
taken over by the Family Life organisation under the
auspices of the Canadian Church Women's Auxiliary, the
largest body of church women in the country. A few
branches and some individual members wished to maintain
the Mothers' Union position on marriage and were linked

to the parent society through the Overseas Department at the Mary Sumner House. Nobody could be happy with a situation which carried within it the seeds of discord and misunderstanding.

New Zealand members were largely responsible for forcing the matter to public debate. Some of their branches had already become impatient with existing regulations and had welcomed any communicant women, whatever their marital status. Hoping to draw in husbands, they called themselves Christian Family Groups.

Those New Zealand members who had stayed within the Mothers' Union framework were determined to push the matter to decision by the whole society. They tabled two resolutions for discussion at the 1968 World-Wide Conference. The first had two parts:

1 that divorced women who had not remarried should be eligible for membership, and

2 that women who, subsequent to their remarriage after divorce, or their marriage to a divorced person, have been admitted or re-admitted to communicant status by the Bishop of the Diocese, should be eligible for membership.

The second resolution proposed that: In view of the present world situation there should be a commonwealth, dominion, or provincial autonomy, and a World Association or World Federation of Mothers' Unions, with the same aim or Objects, but with rules of membership to be decided by their Councils in consultation and agreement with their archbishops and bishops.

Both resolutions were defeated at the World-Wide Conference. An Association of Anglican Women in New Zealand made its appearance the following year which aimed to accommodate all Mothers' Union members, whether they were happy with existing rules of membership or wished to see an extension. As the society officially continued to maintain its existing position, formal connections were severed between the work in New Zealand and the Mary Sumner House.

Australian members watched the New Zealand resolutions closely. As in Canada, their Mothers' Union functioned within a wider body, the Anglican Women of Australia. Church authorities in their province were contemplating new marriage disciplines similar to those in the Church of Canada. In the not too distant future they might find themselves cut off from the main body of the Mothers' Union.

By and large problems in Africa stemmed more from polygamy and 'cattle marriages' than from the effect of divorce courts. Hard cases could arise when a woman who had been given as a bride according to tribal custom was deemed to be not christianly married or where a woman, left with no support for her children when her husband goes to work in the towns and never returns, lives with another man. Some women who were in such ways debarred from membership of the Mothers' Union were outstanding in their devotion to the Church. African women were coming to the conclusion that laws made and maintained in London were not necessarily the best for their very different circumstances.

Although the vote went against the New Zealand resolutions in 1968, one thing became abundantly clear. Differences of opinion existed not only between one country and another but within the membership of each country. Questions were raised about whether the voting membership of the World-Wide Conference reflected the attitudes of the whole society, a sign that full and open discussion of these and related issues was becoming urgent.

New Zealand's second resolution seems to have been originally framed in an attempt to resolve its own difficult situation. They would like all members to accept their suggestions about rules of membership. If this was not possible, might some arrangement be made whereby provinces could stay in the whole body while making their own rules to fit their local Church disciplines? Though this resolution was rejected as the first had been, it started ideas that began to snowball. Autonomy was in the air. It became a positive goal for which many felt they should work. If the Anglican Communion was organised in this way, should not the Mothers' Union do likewise?

It began to seem an inevitable step in the process on which the Mothers' Union was already embarked. In 1968, the year of this World-Wide Conference, newly appointed Mothers' Union workers included a Korean nun, a Chinese woman, two West Indians and several Africans. Was it not right that each province should have the government of its own affairs in its own hands?

While there was no resolution on the subject of organisation, it was obviously causing concern to members. Anyone who embarked on Mothers' Union activity in any sphere beyond the parochial branch entered a labyrinthine system of committees. Deaneries, dioceses and, above all, Mary Sumner House were overgrown thickets of departments and cross-representations. Reports and minutes multiplied. Meetings of one sort and another made heavy demands on the time of voluntary officials.

This system had grown up with the best of intentions, to provide services for members which could flow from the centre through the dioceses. In theory each branch could be linked with the multifarious activities undertaken by the society. Over the years it had worked fairly well but many of those caught up in it were beginning to wonder if it had not become self-perpetuating. Experiment was not easy in such a rigid framework. It underpinned hierarchical attitudes that gave the society a quaintly old-fashioned air. Overhaul was necessary if the Mothers' Union's work was to be efficient in the modern world.

New Zealand had managed to keep a foot in the Mothers' Union door although both its resolutions had been defeated. It had gained a large majority for a further resolution that the three years following 1968 should be regarded as a period of experimentation, during which methods of association should be worked out for the Canadian and New Zealand Mothers' Union.

By this time many in the society were searching for a more radical and hopeful method of tackling problems which had been shown to exist throughout the whole society. A commission was suggested and overwhelmingly approved. Its terms of reference were: 'To examine the Objects of the Mothers' Union and to consider how its witness can be maintained and its work of strengthening Christian family life extended, having in mind that the lifelong nature of marriage is the foundation of family life, and taking into account changes in civil and ecclesiastical law.'

The Executive Committee appointed the present Bishop of Truro, at that time Bishop of Willesden, as chairman. The other members included two lawyers, two clergymen, a woman JP, a woman university lecturer and three Mothers' Union members. Miss Violet Welton was appointed secretary. The Commission began its work in February 1969 and found itself faced with a formidable task. It met for nineteen full sessions of which three were residential. Interviews with witnesses took a further fifteen days and mailbags full of written evidence had to be studied.

Meanwhile an uneasy calm descended on the Mothers' Union. A halt was called to public discussion of issues referred to the Commission but there was plenty of private speculation about what 'they' would say when they finally emerged from the Sinai-cloud that wrapped them from sight as they deliberated.

Three years later the Mothers' Union was presented with the Commission's Report.

NEW DIMENSIONS:
A REPORT IS PRESENTED

THE Report of the Commission, *New Dimensions*, 300 pages long, made complicated reading. It had run into printing troubles and, through no fault of the Commission, made its appearance only a few hours before the Central Council was due to assemble in June 1972 in Manchester to brood over its contents.

Those who heard Bishop Leonard, the Chairman, and other members of the Commission present the report offici- ally to the Mothers' Union were somewhat bleary-eyed, having read it late into the night after arranging to leave their homes for a few days. They were more than a little bemused by what they found there. There was a survey of the historical background of the society, an evaluation of the evidence received by the Commission, a theological appendix and a good deal about the legal implications of attempting to change the Royal Charter.

The section that dealt with the organisation of the Mothers' Union, the departments at the Mary Sumner House, its committee structure and its form of government provided the most challenging reading, full of trenchant criticism and positive suggestions for future action. The overseas chapter was informative and interesting, drawing together many individual strands into a coherent picture.

On the main cause of difference that had originally given birth to the Commission it was immediately obvious that its members had been as unable to reach a unanimous con- clusion as the society itself. On recommendations for future policy, there were two alternative suggestions and a minority report of one which appeared in an appendix. As one alternative had been signed by the chairman and two members of the Commission only, it was in effect another minority report.

The Bishop made the point in his speech to Central Council that in fact the members of the Commission had been agreed on more matters than at first appeared. The three Objects needed re-stating in terms more readily understood by modern readers. Autonomy to a greater or less extent was essential for the work overseas. The society should sponsor Christian Family Groups which would include husbands and wives on equal terms. Radical overhaul of the organisation was essential. On the thorny problem of who could be members, all were agreed that women who were divorced but not re-married must be eligible for membership. Even those who held the strictest view realised that under the 1969 Divorce Reform Act some women might find themselves divorced against their will. The Central Council on this occasion limited its discussion to defining what issues should be referred to affiliated dioceses for study among members during the following twelve months.

The Aims and Objects set out in the 1926 Charter must obviously be revised but no-one present seemed particularly pleased with the form of words suggested by the Commission. Autonomy was right and necessary but its implications needed to be grasped and defined. In particular, did the granting of autonomy mean that a province had the power to frame its own rules of membership, rules which might be different in some respects from those in the 1926 Constitution? This might mean that in future the Central Council would make decisions on such matters only for the United Kingdom and for those provinces which chose to accept its rulings.

Every member everywhere was asked to study the alternatives that had been proposed by the Commission and to decide for herself what she felt would be right. Out of such study and debate it was hoped that a common mind would emerge.

The representatives went home to get the talking started. The tone had been set for the process by the Chaplain to the Mothers' Union, John Hughes, Bishop of Croydon. During the years he has held the office he has followed the affairs of the society closely and has found the right word to meet its particular need on many occasions. During the discussions in Manchester he gave an address at Compline that stressed the way a Christian body should tackle decision-making. 'The fact is that in the New Testament the Holy Spirit of truth strikes truth out of the group that explores the way of truth *together*, as I have personally proved time and time again. Truth comes in and through the reality of *meeting*— in what the New Testament calls the *koinonia*—fellowship— communion—participation.'

The floodgates were opened at last and pent-up views and opinions poured out. Some found long-held beliefs re-inforced. Others embarked on the painful process of having their minds changed in the light of the evidence presented to them. In many places church halls and private houses echoed to words like autonomy and Alternative B, minority reports and constitutional implications. There was a feeling of excitement that something was going to happen at last to give new impetus to the work of the Mothers' Union but it was tinged with apprehension. When opposing views were strongly held, someone was bound to suffer when matters were forced to a decision. From the welter of words and ideas, resolutions emerged to set the framework for the dis-cussions at the Central Council meetings held at the Royal Holloway College in Surrey in the summer of 1973.

Between the setting up of the Commission and its reporting Mrs Hallifax had laid down her office as Central President during which she had seen some of the most difficult years in the society's life. She had been succeeded by Mrs Susan

Varah. Mrs Llewellyn-Davies had also retired as Central
Secretary, after many years of distinguished and devoted
work for the cause of marriage and family life which had
earned her the respect of many within and without the
Mothers' Union.

With Mrs Varah in the chair the Central Council started
on re-wording the aim of the society, necessary if a new
Charter was to be applied for. It arrived at: The advance-
ment of the Christian religion in the sphere of marriage and
family life.

The Commission's Report had recommended that the
original three objects should be extended to five. Four new
suggestions for the wording of these five objects had been
submitted for discussion along with a resolution that the
original three objects be retained. Out of such complication
the Central Council produced five objects:

1 To uphold our Lord's teaching on the nature of marriage.
2 To encourage parents to bring up their children in the
   faith of the Church.
3 To maintain a world-wide fellowship of those united in
   prayer, worship and service.
4 To promote conditions in society favourable to stable
   homes and happy childhood.
5 To help those whose family life has met with adversity.

The Press was specially delighted with the third of the
new objects. A world-wide fellowship of *those*—nothing
about women. Were fathers to be let in to the Mothers'
Union? Equality indeed! In fact the society had decided not
to close any doors unnecessarily. There might come a time
when men would seek to share the work for family life and
happy marriage. The way was being left open for them.

There was still a need for a phrase, something that summed
up in a few words what the society tries to do. So appeared—
The Purpose: To be specially concerned with all that
strengthens and preserves family life.

The only question that was raised about granting

autonomy to those provinces who asked for it was how soon it could come into effect. Members in the United Kingdom were eager for it to be given. African delegates welcomed the chance to tackle their problems freely, while keeping in fellowship with the rest of the society. Australia heaved a sigh of relief. Canada's response when autonomy was fully granted was simply. 'Thnak you. Now we are back in.'

It was obvious that the new relationship between parts of the whole society would mean new methods of making decisions for the whole. Colonel Draper, who with Mr Nugee, another member of the Commission, had always been available to give help on legal and constitutional matters, remarked at this point that the Constitution had been inherited from an age which did not use aircraft. A pattern was suggested of a triennial World-Wide Conference which would move round the world, meeting each time in a different country. The feeling was that fellowship among members would grow and deepen as the tight organisational bonds were loosened.

Central Council embarked soberly on proposals concerning regulations about membership, aware that this issue might well be a rock of division among members of the fellowship. Although the acceptance of full autonomy meant that decisions taken by this Central Council would now apply only to the home country, they would obviously be of the greatest importance to the future of the whole movement.

There were several resolutions before Central Council. Some had suggested that there should be no change at all in qualifications for membership. Some wanted membership extended to those who were divorced but had not remarried. Some held that those who had been admitted to communion after a second marriage should also be allowed in to the Mothers' Union. An idea was put forward that an associate membership be created for those at present barred from joining. Finally it was suggested that all baptised women who are prepared to support the objects of the society be admitted without any qualifications about their own marital position.

When the issues had been set before the Central Council, the Bishop of Croydon suggested that the vote be conducted in prayerful silence. The result when it was received in a silence equally intense was startling. Two hundred and fifty-four of those voting were in favour of extending membership to all who were prepared to accept the society's objects, whatever their own marital status. Only 49 votes were cast in favour of all the other proposals that had been made. The Mothers' Union had decided that the time was ripe to change the emphasis to the principles for which it stood and to leave decisions as to who should seek membership to the applicants themselves.

As to the society's place in the Anglican Communion, the general feeling was that for the moment the closest links should be maintained. Ordinary membership, which had never been limited to communicants, was now defined as open to all those who have been baptised in the name of the Holy Trinity and declare their support for the aims and objects of the society. Official workers, a term which was in future to include Enrolling Members but not members of branch committees, must be communicant members of the Church of England or a Church in communion with it.

The Commission had laid great emphasis on the need for Christian Family Groups, some of its members suggesting that their development might well become the main work undertaken by the Mothers' Union in the future. Central Council agreed that work among families as a whole was urgently necessary and undertook to examine ways in which it could be developed. It remained unconvinced that the best way would be to launch such a venture on a large scale at once. Out of the re-appraisal of all aspects of Mothers' Union work that had become necessary as the result of *New Dimensions* and the subsequent discussions fresh opportunities might arise. Something like family groups might well snowball and spread as the Mothers' Union itself had grown from a small meeting in a country parish to the world-wide fellowship that had been striking out in new directions almost a hundred years later.

Even in the joy of renewal, members could not escape some sadness. Among their ranks were the minority who felt that the decisions that had been taken on the membership issue were a betrayal of what the society had been raised up to do. Its witness to life-long marriage would, they considered, be nullified by opening its ranks to those who appeared to deny it in their own lives. They suggested that, if a majority wishes these changes, the Mothers' Union should be closed down and a new organisation be set up with new rules.

The majority could not agree. A delegate from Guyana spoke for most of those present when she talked of the value she placed on the way her own mother had brought her up though she herself had departed from it in some respects when bringing up her own children. 'But we have not abandoned her standards; we have simply changed our methods, and are trying to use the best ones for our own generation. Do not deprive us of the support and heritage of the Mothers' Union.'

FOOTNOTE

Centenary 1976

FROM time to time the Mothers' Union has contemplated changing its name. The difficulty is always that, while there are many who are not happy with it, nobody ever comes up with an acceptable alternative.

When the Central Council was considering *New Dimensions* in 1972, the question came up again. Colonel Draper explained the legal implications of such a step and added that the Commission had studied the matter carefully but did not consider the case for change proved. 'It is a name of which nobody has any cause to be ashamed.' The Mothers' Union was certainly in no mood to be ashamed as it set out on its work of implementing the decisions it had taken in 1973.

Tentative plans soon appeared for new ventures. A parish that already had an afternoon branch and an evening group launched a Christian Family Group which drew fifty people to its inaugural meeting even though the Prime Minister had inconveniently arranged an election for the following day. An unexpected spin-off was the feeling of renewed life in the two existing meetings.

The Church of England Men's Society in one diocese collaborated with the Mothers' Union in drawing up courses for discussion at joint parents' meetings. As the society has now pledged itself explicitly to help those whose family life has met with adversity the Company of Compassion is looking forward to increased practical support for its work.

Heartened by the sympathetic press coverage of recent

developments, the Mothers' Union is beginning to pay more attention to communicating its message. A diocese appointed a Publicity Officer who set about training herself for the job. Another has been offered a monthly column in the diocesan newspaper.

The Mary Sumner House has been busy implementing decisions taken. A Supplementary Charter was overwhelmingly accepted at a thousand-strong Extraordinary General Meeting and approved by the Queen. She, with Queen Elizabeth the Queen Mother, agreed to continue as patrons. The Duchess of Kent also accepted an invitation to become patron. The Mothers' Union prayer has been put in more modern language. There are new membership cards, a revised admission service and several explanatory leaflets and promotional literature.

An Education Department has been established at the Mary Sumner House, incorporating three former departments, backed by a resource centre to help branches in their work. The Young Members' Department is exploring its new role, 'free to experiment with whatever type of group would be most viable in any one locality or situation; young wives' groups, ad hoc discussion groups, fringe groups, mother and baby groups, play groups, pram groups, etc.' It will no doubt be paying a great deal of attention to the position of fathers in its work.

More changes are in the pipe-line.

The Central President has been off on her travels. In the space of three weeks she visited Canada, Eire and Wales. She was present when the Canadian Mothers' Union voted to accept fully the new aims and objects and set about re-building unity among their members.

The Church of Ireland Gazette carried a leader about her visit there. 'The Mothers' Union possesses an infinite capacity for survival,' it began and continued: 'Her tour, it seems, was something in the nature of a triumphal procession, culminating in a service in Christ Church Cathedral,

Dublin, which taxed the capacity of one of our largest buildings. Clearly, her audiences came not to hear an apologia for the actions of the Central Council or because controversy was in the air, but simply to join in an act of worship with someone who held the highest office in their Union. Such solidarity demands that so powerful and numerous an organisation of the Church be treated with the utmost seriousness and this capacity to influence for good be fully utilised. We make bold to say that there is scarcely another office-bearer within the Anglican Communion who could command such audiences, a fact which in itself is food for thought.'

A few months later Mrs Varah was in Malawi, sharing discussions on an autonomous future and meeting yet more of the African members who have been special friends of all Central Presidents. Perhaps Mrs Varah is held in particular veneration for she is the mother of triplet sons, an achievement they treat with due respect.

At home the Mothers' Union tackled problems on its doorstep. It studied the abortion issue and probed into the current interest in the occult. It turned its attention to battered wives and one-parent families. The community relations officer in Manchester started a social club for Asian women and ran holiday play schemes for the children. More children in need of homes were fostered by Mothers' Union members.

Some Australian homes were hit by devastating floods. Members there worked long hours to help the homeless. Some lost everything themselves. The Overseas Fund sent £1,000 to the Commonwealth President for use at her discretion.

Finance proved an increasing worry. In 1973 expenditure exceeded income by £23,000. Economies are being made wherever possible and members are having to give more to keep the work going. Mrs Anne Hopkinson was also concerned with money. She represented the Mothers' Union at a conference on the effect of inflation on lower-paid families with young children. It asked the Government to raise the family allowance to £2 and to give this to each child, including the first.

Birthdays are in the air. Jo Roberts, a Mothers' Union worker in Korea, was sixty, a day to be specially honoured by the tradition of that country. Everyone seems to have overlooked that she was not Korean born, perhaps because she has largely forgotten that fact herself. She sat in the sanctuary at a crowded Sung Eucharist wearing a traditional Korean dress of yellow-cream silk.

'After the Eucharist, she was escorted to an awning set up on a level space below the church and in front of the priest's house, and under which on straw matting was a long low table piled high with Korean cakes and fruit. Sitting cross-legged on a cushion and facing the assembled crowd across the goodies, she was supported by a bishop and senior priest on either side. Then she was offered cups of wine. Traditionally this would have been done by children and grandchildren, but, in lieu of these, they were offered by a procession of children and women whom she had helped. There were some whose legs and feet are now usable but not supple enough to bend, and others too small to allow them to pour and present the wine cup across the table while kneeling, and they by dispensation stood to do this. Fortunately, the one thus honoured is only required to taste each cup and a large bowl is placed beforehand out of sight under the table to take the remainder!'

The whole Mothers' Union is preparing for its centenary. There will be great services and meetings throughout the world. The fellowship has been renewed and will be giving thanks for its heritage while it looks to work and witness in the future.

INDEX

Change in Focus